The
WHITE HOUSE
CHRISTMAS MYSTERY

CAROLE MARSH
MYSTERIES

by
Carole Marsh

Managing Editor: Sherry Moss
Editorial Assistant: Erin S. Kelly
Cover Design: Vicki DeJoy
Picture Credits: Amanda McCutcheon
Content Design: Steven St. Laurent, Lynette Rowe

Gallopade is proud to be a member and supporter of these educational organizations and associations:

American Booksellers Association
International Reading Association
National Association for Gifted Children
The National School Supply and Equipment Association
The National Council for the Social Studies
Museum Store Association
Association of Partners for Public Lands

VISIT THE CAROLE MARSH MYSTERIES WEBSITE

www.carolemarshmysteries.com

- *Check out what's coming up next! Are we coming to your area with our next book release? Maybe you can have your book signed by the author!*

- *Join the Carole Marsh Mysteries Fan Club!*

- *Apply for the chance to be a character in an upcoming Carole Marsh Mystery!*

- *Learn how to write your own mystery!*

THE CAROLE MARSH MYSTERIES SERIES

What Kids Say About Carole Marsh Mysteries . . .

I love the real locations! Reading the book always makes me want to go and visit them all on our next family vacation. My Mom says maybe, but I can't wait!

One day, I want to be a real kid in one of Ms. Marsh's mystery books. I think it would be fun, and I think I am a real character anyway. I filled out the application and sent it in and am keeping my fingers crossed!

History was not my favorite subject till I starting reading Carole Marsh Mysteries. Ms. Marsh really brings history to life. Also, she leaves room for the scary and fun.

I think Christina is so smart and brave. She is lucky to be in the mystery books because she gets to go to a lot of places. I always wonder just how much of the book is true and what is made up. Trying to figure that out is fun!

Grant is cool and funny! He makes me laugh a lot!!

I like that there are boys and girls in the story of different ages. Some mysteries I outgrow, but I can always find a favorite character to identify with in these books.

They are scary, but not too scary. They are funny. I learn a lot.
There is always food which makes me hungry. I feel like I am there.

What Adults Say About Carole Marsh Mysteries . . .

I think kids love these books because they have such a wealth of detail.
I know I learn a lot reading them! It's an engaging way to look at the
history of any place or event. I always say I'm only going to read one
chapter to the kids, but that never happens—it's always two or three, at
least! —Librarian

Reading the mystery and going on the field trip—Scavenger Hunt in
hand—was the most fun our class ever had! It really brought the place
and its history to life. They loved the real kids characters and all the
humor. I loved seeing them learn that reading is an experience to
enjoy! —4th grade teacher

Carole Marsh is really on to something with these unique mysteries.
They are so clever; kids want to read them all. The Teacher's Guides
are chock full of activities, recipes, and additional fascinating
information. My kids thought I was an expert on the subject—and
with this tool, I felt like it! —3rd grade teacher

My students loved writing their own Real Kids/Real Places mystery
book! Ms. Marsh's reproducible guidelines are a real jewel. They
learned about copyright and more & ended up with their own book
they were so proud of! —Reading/Writing Teacher

This book is dedicated with love to my aunt, who gave me my first big chance. I appreciate your trust in me. Thank you to my mother and father for providing me with unconditional love, a deluxe education, a strong faith, and a steadfast work ethic. Special thanks to Mr. Michael Robert Johnson. I am grateful for the vast amount of knowledge you have shared.

-ESK

This book is a complete work of fiction. All events are fictionalized, and although the first names of real children are used, their characterization in this book is fiction.

For additional information on Carole Marsh Mysteries, visit:
www.carolemarshmysteries.com

Is the answer down there?

20 YEARS AGO ...

As a mother and an author, one of the fondest periods of my life was when I decided to write mystery books for children. At this time (1979) kids were pretty much glued to the TV, something parents and teachers complained about the way they do about video games today.

I decided to set each mystery in a real place—a place kids could go and visit for themselves after reading the book. And I also used real children as characters. Usually a couple of my own children served as characters, and I had no trouble recruiting kids from the book's location to also be characters.

Also, I wanted all the kids—boys and girls of all ages—to participate in solving the mystery. And, I wanted kids to learn something as they read. Something about the history of the location. And I wanted the stories to be funny.

That formula of real+scary+smart+fun served me well. The kids and I had a great time visiting each site and many of the events in the stories actually came out of our experiences there. (For example, we really did take a private tour of the White House!)

I love getting letters from teachers and parents who say they read the book with their class or child, then visited the historic site and saw all the places in the mystery for themselves. What's so great about that? What's great is that you and your children have an experience that bonds you together forever. Something you shared. Something you both cared about at the time. Something that crossed all age levels—a good story, a good scare, a good laugh!

20 years later,

Carole Marsh

**Christina
Yother**   **Grant
Yother**   **Candace
Mack**   **Riondra
Mack**

About the Characters

Christina Yother, 9, from Peachtree City, Georgia

Grant Yother, 7, from Peachtree City, Georgia, Christina's brother

Candace Mack as April, 11, from Peachtree City, Georgia

Riondra Mack as Denise Claire ("D.C."), 8, April's sister, from Peachtree City, Georgia

Although tours of the White House were suspended indefinitely following September 11, 2001, you can contact your Congressperson to arrange a tour.

Titles in the Carole Marsh Mysteries Series

Books and Teacher's Guides are available at booksellers, libraries, school supply stores, museums, and many other locations!

CONTENTS

1 'TIS THE SEASON TO BE ... BORED?!

Christina stared through the big bay window in her grandmother Mimi's living room. She sighed, watching the rain that pelted the scraggly bushes and dull brown grass. What a dreary December day! Her younger brother Grant contentedly played with his Matchbox cars under Mimi's glorious gold and white Christmas tree. He could amuse himself anywhere, Christina thought jealously. She was tired of reading, tired of playing, and most of all, tired of school!

"Why don't we call your friends April and D.C. and ask them to come visit for a while?" asked Papa, Christina and Grant's grandfather.

"OMKHAY!" exclaimed Grant, whose mouth was full of gingerbread cookie.

Papa went to call April and D.C.'s mother while

Mimi's
House

Visiting
Friends

Christina stared at the sparkling white lights on the Christmas tree. They reminded her of stars in the winter sky. She made a wish on one of them . . . for something exciting to happen.

"Hello!" shouted April as she dashed through the front door. She dragged D.C. by the hand behind her.

"Boy, is it ever wet out there," said D.C. "I don't see why we get rain instead of having snow like everyone else in the country." The big story in the news was the blizzard that was blanketing much of the nation in snow.

As D.C. finished speaking, the phone rang, and Christina ran to answer it. "Hello?" she said.

A stern, very official-sounding voice asked for her grandmother. "It's for you, Mimi," she said, handing her the phone. Christina wondered whom the stern voice belonged to and why they were calling Mimi. She went and sat down at the big white kitchen table where Grant, April, D.C., and Papa were starting a card game of Go Fish.

Mimi rushed into the kitchen with a huge grin on her face. "It's final!" she exclaimed.

"What's final?" Christina and Grant asked at the same time.

Mimi's House

Visiting Friends

"Our private tour of the White House!" exclaimed Mimi. She continued, "I'm planning to write a book about the White House, and Papa and I planned a tour so I could do some research. We thought it would be a fun Christmas surprise for us to take you and Grant along. You can each bring a friend along to Washington, D.C."

Christina and Grant looked at April and D.C. "You want to come, don't you?" Christina asked.

"D.C. is going to D.C.," sang Grant.

"You silly!" said Christina. "By the way, what does D.C. stand for?" she asked.

"It stands for Denise Claire," explained D.C. "I was born in Washington D.C., so my parents gave me a nickname that matched the place were I was born."

"D.C. also stands for the District of Columbia, the name chosen for America's capital city. The land for the city was taken from the states of Maryland and Virginia," Christina said in her *I know everything* voice.

Grant didn't respond by poking fun at his sister's typical know-it-all sort of statement. He looked crestfallen. "But what about school?" he asked downheartedly. "Christmas vacation doesn't start for another week."

"Your Mom and I have already settled it with the school," said Mimi. "The principal approved your absences

Visiting
Friends

Going to
D.C.!

because your trip will be an educational one."

"IPPHHHEE!" shouted Grant, who was eating gingerbread again. He even had crumbs in his head full of white-blond ringlets.

"We leave in four days, so start packing your bags!" said Papa.

Christina didn't hear him because she was daydreaming about the trip. Her wish for something exciting had come true! Only she hoped that the trip wouldn't be TOO exciting. Every time she and Grant went on a trip with Mimi, they ended up getting sucked into a real-life mystery. She hoped this trip would be in the Christmas spirit and not involve any other types of spirits . . . or ghosts . . . or missing people–especially not anyone like–say–Santa Claus!

Going to
D.C.!

Pack Your
Bags!

2 Over the River and Through the Clouds

"Bye!" Grant said as he waved to the rapidly shrinking crowd peering out of a series of windows at Atlanta's Hartsfield International Airport.

Christina felt a twitching in the pit of her stomach. The feeling of the plane pulling away from the earth and rising into the sky always gave her goosebumps. She stared out the window at the snowflakes whizzing past as the plane rose above the bank of blizzard-laden clouds. Her thoughts were interrupted by D.C.'s voice.

" . . . and I hope we get to see Gramps while we're in the White House," she said to April.

"Your grandfather *lives* in the White House?" asked Grant skeptically.

"No, he *works* there as a Secret Service agent," replied April.

Atlanta, Georgia

Washington, D.C.

"Wow, he's a real-life spy!" exclaimed Grant, drawing the wrong conclusion.

"Not quite," said D.C. with a smile. "He gives tours and makes sure that the house remains safe for the First Family."

"The movie's about to start," Papa informed the children. "It should last until we're ready to land at Dulles Airport." As everyone settled back in their seats and put on their headphones, Christina thought about what the trip would hold for Mimi and Papa and the four friends. Certainly history. Hopefully–mystery!

Clunk! The jolt of the plane's landing gear moving into position jarred Christina awake. "Boy, you sure missed a good movie," April informed her. Christina rubbed the sleep out of her blue-gray October eyes–as her great-grandfather, Boom Pa, called them.

"Time to go! Make sure you have all of your stuff," Mimi said, as everyone got ready to leave the plane. Amid the holiday hustle and bustle of the airport, the kids could see the snow rapidly accumulating outside.

"Looks like the folks in Washington might get to have a real white Christmas," said Papa as he swung the

Atlanta,
Georgia

Washington,
D.C.

gang's suitcases off the rotating conveyor belt in the terminal. "Let's go hail a cab so we can get settled in the hotel."

After arriving at the Willard Hotel in downtown Washington, Christina, April, and D.C. found, to their delight, that they would get to share a hotel room of their own. Grant, however, was not so thrilled. He was going to stay with Mimi and Papa in order to "keep his head on straight," as Papa would say.

When the three girls arrived at their room, Christina couldn't help noticing that the number on the door was 1313. She hoped that it wasn't bad luck or something sinister like that.

April opened the door and rushed into the room. "Wow, look at this place!" she exclaimed. D.C.'s soft brown eyes became wide with awe as she gazed around the luxurious chamber. There were three beds, each covered in a dark blue velvet spread with loads of fluffy burgundy pillows. A festive green Christmas garland was strung around the top of the room. A huge window surrounded by heavy forest green draperies overlooked downtown Washington. Christina noticed that the snow was still falling in large, soft clumps.

She heard April calling from the bathroom. She and

Washington. D.C.

Willard Hotel

D.C. peeked through the door and spied a gigantic bathtub. "You could keep an octopus in this thing!" cried D.C.

Christina grimaced and gave her a *no-way* look. She wasn't fond of creepy, crawly, squishy things.

Just as Christina was contemplating the unappetizing idea of an eight-armed creature swimming in her bath water, Mimi knocked on the door. "Meet us in the lobby for dinner in five minutes!" she said.

Washington.
D.C.

Willard
Hotel

3 MOTORCADE MADNESS

As the whole group piled into the taxi, April called their attention to a large group of black vehicles traveling close together at a snail's pace. There was a police escort in front and back with blue lights flashing, illuminating the darkened street.

"That's some kind of traffic jam," mused Grant. "All of those people have the same cars."

"That's not just any old traffic jam," Papa explained. "That's the presidential motorcade. The First Family is on its way to Camp David to spend Christmas vacation." Everyone watched in awe as the intimidating procession of vehicles crawled slowly through an intersection. They didn't even stop for red lights.

"You mean the President is actually *in there* somewhere?" Grant asked in amazement.

Willard
Hotel

A Traffic
Jam?

"Yep, he rides in a special presidential Cadillac parade limousine," said Papa. "All of those black Chevrolet Suburbans are filled with Secret Service agents who protect the president and his family."

"Hey, D.C., is your grandfather in one of those cars?" Grant asked.

"No, he stays in the White House," D.C. replied, smiling. "There are two kinds of Secret Service agents— uniformed and plainclothes. Uniformed agents stay at the White House and give tours. Plainclothes agents are assigned to protect the first family. They often travel with the president. Our grandfather is a uniformed agent. But he knows some of the people who are assigned to protect the president when he travels," she added proudly.

The cab pulled slowly out into traffic. "We're going to take a driving tour of the city before we eat," said Mimi. The children paid close attention as the cabby drove past famous Washington buildings, such as the Kennedy Center for the Performing Arts, the Lincoln Memorial, the Jefferson Memorial, the Washington Monument, and the U.S. Capitol.

April said, "Boy, Washington sure is a confusing city!"

"I know!" exclaimed Grant. "The streets are like

A Traffic Jam?

No! A Motorcade!

alphabet soup!" he added, referring to the fact that some streets in Washington are named with letters instead of numbers or names.

"Well, here we are at the restaurant," said Papa as the taxi pulled up at a place called Old Ebbitt Grill. It was across from the White House.

As everyone got out of the taxi, Christina noticed a group of trucks going in the opposite direction of the presidential motorcade. These trucks were also moving at a slow pace and traveling in a group, but they were towing what looked like animal trailers. They pulled up to the East Gate of the White House and a guard waved them through. Christina wondered why anyone would want to transport a bunch of animals to the White House.

The group piled out of the cab into the flurrying snow. Christina stood distractedly on the sidewalk, staring in the direction of the White House. She was still puzzled by the motorcade of animal trailers that she had just seen.

"Come on, let's go in. I'm starved!" April exclaimed as she grabbed Christina's hand and pulled her into the restaurant.

Old Ebbitt Grill was very beautiful inside. Candlelight flickered off the rich mahogany bar, the white tablecloths, and the freshly cut flowers set at each table.

Mimi told the children to look for famous politicians. Many of Washington's prominent figures dined regularly at Old Ebbitt.

The hostess seated the group at a table by a window with a fabulous view of the White House. Christina's eyes widened as she watched the white snowflakes drift down peacefully from the heavens. It looked like a storybook picture. Just then, the waiter arrived with their food.

"Let's eat!" said Papa.

"First, let's have a toast to our private White House tour," said Mimi. "We were lucky to get security clearance with the tightened regulations after the September 11 terrorist attacks. And after all, this is a celebration dinner!" Everyone raised their glasses of sweet tea and clinked them together.

After a scrumptious dinner, the kids, Mimi, and Papa took a taxi back to the hotel. They were all full and sleepy. Grant snoozed against Mimi's furry coat while the girls chattered excitedly about their very own private tour of the White House that was scheduled for tomorrow–Christmas Eve!

When they reached the hotel, everyone headed

Old Ebbitt
Grill

Look At The
White House!

groggily back to their rooms. Papa had to carry Grant into the hotel because he didn't wake up, even when the cold snowflakes outside the cab fell on his face. After saying goodnights and settling into bed, Christina fell asleep with visions of sugarplums–and Secret Service agents–dancing in her head.

Look At The
White House!

Back To
Willard Hotel

4 I'M DREAMING OF A WHITE... HOUSE!

"WAKE UP!!" shouted April and D.C. in unison, jumping up and down on Christina's bed. Christina opened her eyes and stared at them through a sleepy fog.

"Okay, I'm awake," she said, smiling. "You guys are raising the dead!" Wow, I hope they're not *really* raising the dead, Christina thought. That's creepy!

Today was the big day of the private White House tour. Everyone met for breakfast in the hotel lobby. "Are we ready for this?" asked Mimi, as they ordered.

"Truthfully, I'm a little nervous," said April.

"I'm not!" said D.C. "I hope we get to see Gramps today."

"I'm just plain hungry!" said Grant, rubbing his

Time To
Get Up!

Let's Eat
Breakfast!

stomach in anticipation of warm waffles and syrup.

Christina didn't say anything. She was still a little spooked by her *raising the dead* comment. She had an uneasy feeling about this trip, what with the 1313 on the hotel room door, thinking about dead people, and the mysterious motorcade the group had witnessed last night. I will not let this trip turn into mystery-solving mayhem, thought Christina, between bites of a delicious Belgian waffle topped with whipped cream.

After breakfast, Mimi, Papa, and the kids walked to the White House. It wasn't snowing that morning, but five or so inches of snow had accumulated during the night, and the weather forecast was calling for more snow before nightfall.

"Old Man Winter really has it in for the Capital City, doesn't he?" Papa observed.

"I'm surprised the whole city didn't have to shut down," said D.C.

"The maintenance crews must have worked very hard last night to keep the streets in driving condition. After all, it would be very inconvenient if the capital of the United States had to shut down," said Mimi.

"Yeah, 'cause if the city shut down, then you would have to shut down, right, D.C.?" Grant said jokingly.

Let's Eat Breakfast!

To The White House!

"Oh, stop it," D.C. replied, sticking out her tongue at Grant.

"Quit acting like such kids," Christina admonished in her schoolteacher voice. "You have to behave in the White House, or they'll kick us all out. Besides, you wouldn't want the President to catch you looking undignified, would you?"

"Dignified-shmignified," Grant said disgustedly. "Who cares?"

"We're here!" shouted Mimi excitedly. "Let's go!"

Mimi and Papa herded the kids towards the entrance to the colonnade. A stern uniformed guard asked for their names and then handed them special badges to wear around their necks. Before the guard could introduce the group to its tour guide, April and D.C. ran up to the man, hugging him and shouting, "Gramps! Gramps!"

"It's okay, these are my grandkids," he said, nodding to the other guard, who had a bewildered expression on his face. "My name is Edgar," he said, addressing the rest of the group. "I wanted to surprise April and D.C., so I arranged to be your tour guide. Speaking of that, let's go!" The group happily moved forward, led by Edgar with April

To The
White House!

Hey, It's
Gramps!

and D.C. on either side of him.

"As we walk, I'll tell you some background information about the White House. Our first president, George Washington, had the idea to plan a capital city and a residence for the president. He chose a French architect named Pierre L'Enfant and an African American named Benjamin Banneker to survey and design the city. An Irish-born architect named James Hoban won a contest to become the designer of the president's house."

Edgar kept walking and talking, never taking a breath. Christina could tell he had memorized his historical speech years and years ago.

"The building of the White House began in 1792 and was completed in 1800. British troops set fire to the house in 1814. Most of the original frame was left standing, so the house was rebuilt around these timbers. It was because of the fire that the White House earned its name. The finished structure was painted white to disguise the marks and stains left by the smoke. Today the house serves several functions, such as a home for the president and his family, an office for the president and many of his most important employees, and a museum to house valuable historical objects, such as the furniture and art that you will see in each room on the tour."

Hey, It's
Cramps!

Let's Take
A Tour

Wow! Look at this place!

Edgar continued his wordy speech. "The president is the Chief Executive Officer of our country, meaning that he is the most powerful leader. He has the final say on all government decisions. He also represents our country when it comes to America's relationships with other nations. He is the one who decides when we should go to war, what to do with the country's budget, and many other important decisions. He doesn't do all of this by himself though. He has a very special group of advisors called the Cabinet. I'll tell you more about that later."

The kids listened to Edgar drone on with more facts about the President and White House history as he led the group through the East Colonnade and up the stairs into the huge East Room. Edgar explained that this room was used for press conferences and state functions because its large size could accommodate many people.

"Back in the days when John Adams was president, wet laundry was hung in the East Room so it wouldn't be seen on the White House lawn," said Edgar.

Christina turned to D.C. and whispered, "Your grandfather is nice, but he sure does talk a lot."

"You can say that again," D.C. whispered back, giggling.

Edgar pointed out the priceless portrait of George

Let's Take
A Tour

Here's The
East Room

Washington that hung to the left of the fireplace. "This portrait is the only item that has been in the White House since it was built," Edgar explained. "When the White House was set on fire by British troops in 1814, Dolley Madison, President James Madison's wife, risked her life to rescue this painting."

The kids stared at the lifelike portrait with awe. The great George Washington seemed to gaze into the distance with serious, but kind, eyes.

"He looks like he's wearing *makeup*," Grant whispered, referring to the first president's very pink cheeks. The rest of the group frowned at him while Christina wondered how he could take such a serious moment so lightly.

The tour moved on to the next stop, the beautiful Green Room. The walls were covered in a shimmering pale green wallpaper, and an ornate Oriental rug covered the floor. A glittering chandelier with millions of sparkly crystals was suspended from the ceiling. A portrait of Benjamin Franklin hung over the fireplace. The group listened attentively as Edgar explained that many of the pieces of silver in the room had belonged to past presidents and their families. Christina took one last look at the Green Room as the group moved through the Cross Hall,

Here's The
East Room

The Gorgeous
Green Room!

which ran from the East Room to the State Dining Room.

The next destination was the beautiful Blue Room. Everyone gasped in admiration of the stunning scene. The children felt surrounded by the elaborate furniture upholstered in satiny blue fabric and embroidered in gold thread with eagles and swirly designs. A huge blue spruce Christmas tree, cut from deep in the forests of West Virginia, stood in the center of the room. The tree soared to the ceiling, and was covered in fancy ornaments. A sign announced the theme of this year's decorations: ANIMALS OF THE WHITE HOUSE PAST.

Christina noticed that there seemed to be a uniformed Secret Service agent posted in each room. She assumed that their job was to keep people from breaking things and sitting on furniture. Not that she would ever *dream* of doing that anyway.

Edgar pointed out the room's oval shape and explained that George Washington had a fondness for oval rooms, resulting in the shape of the Blue Room and the famous Oval Office. "If you look out the windows, you can see a nice view of the Washington Monument," Edgar said, ushering them towards a window covered in blue satin drapes. Christina noticed that the snow was starting to fall faster and heavier.

The Gorgeous
Green Room!

The Beautiful
Blue Room

Edgar led his guests into the striking Red Room. The walls were painted a deep shade of red with a gold border near the ceiling. Lots of elaborate red and gold furniture was grouped around the fireplace. A portrait of Dolley Madison, the famous and popular Washington hostess, hung on the wall. Edgar explained that in President and Mrs. James Madison's day, the room had been painted yellow and was used for receptions.

"Whoa, check out this couch!" Grant shouted, waving the others over to his side of the room. "The legs on this thing look like giant fish!"

Indeed they did, thought Christina. The couch sat on intricate legs made of blackish wood carved to look like fish scales finished with gold fish heads and fins. They were kind of scary looking, like something from a Greek mythology book.

Edgar smiled and said, "That's a very special piece of American furniture. The dolphin feet are very unusual."

"Dolphin feet? They look like plain old fish to me," said Grant.

Christina looked out the window through the room's thick gold drapes. The snow was falling much harder now, and she could barely see outside. The ground was covered with what looked like almost a foot of snow. *I hope we can*

The Beautiful
Blue Room

The Resplendent
Red Room

get back to the hotel, she thought as she followed Edgar, Mimi, and Papa into the next room.

"Normally, we would stop by the State Dining Room," said Edgar, as he led them past some closed doors. "But a meal is being prepared for the First Family, so it's off-limits this morning."

"That reminds me," said Mimi. "After the tour, let's go somewhere for lunch."

"Okay," said Papa in agreement. "Everybody meet at the East Gate at noon."

"Well, that's the end of the tour just now," said Edgar. "The second floor is now off-limits to guests. It contains the Lincoln Bedroom, which President Lincoln used as his office, the Yellow Oval Room, which is used by the President and First Lady to hold formal receptions, the Queen's Bedroom, where visiting foreign dignitaries stay, and the First Family's private bedrooms, living areas, and studies. Other sections of the White House include the West Wing, where the Oval Office and the Cabinet Room are located. At the moment, these sections are closed for the holiday season."

"Thank you very much for the tour," Mimi said gratefully to Edgar.

"You're more than welcome," he graciously

The Resplendent
Red Room

Back Into
Cross Hall

responded. "If you have any more questions, please feel free to come and ask me. I'll be at the front entrance."

"Bye, Gramps! We love you!" said D.C. and April, giving Edgar big hugs.

"I'll see you again before you leave," said Edgar, smiling. They watched him head back down the Cross Hall.

Back Into Cross Hall

To The East Room

5 NO MORE GRANT

The group slowly wandered back to the East Room. Once they arrived there, Christina noticed that the four kids had fallen behind Mimi and Papa. The adults didn't seem to have noticed. Suddenly April tapped Christina on the shoulder. "Where's Grant?" she asked nervously.

"You don't see him?" Christina replied. She glanced around the vast expanse of the East Room, and sure enough, there was no sign of Grant. Oh great, she thought. That's all I need is to lose my little brother on Christmas Eve. "Maybe we should go look for . . ."

She didn't get to finish her sentence. April and D.C. gasped in horror as two hands reached out of the wall and pulled Christina behind it. The two girls followed, hoping to save their friend. Once they were behind the wall, they heard Grant snicker and say, "Gotcha!"

To The East Room

Behind The Walls

27

When their eyes adjusted to the dark, the girls could barely see Grant standing in a small room that looked like a closet. A tiny window high up on the wall let in a small amount of light. "Look what I found! It's a secret door in the wall!" Grant whispered excitedly.

"Uh-oh, I bet we're not supposed to be in here. If anyone finds us, we'll be in major trouble," said D.C. worriedly. "I wonder if anyone saw us go in."

"So what do we do now?" April asked.

"I guess we should see if we can find a way out of here," said Christina. "Wait, what's this?" She stooped and picked up a small white square of paper off of the floor. She turned it over and read:

This place

is a zoo.

Behind The
Walls

Surely Not
A Clue!

"It looks to me like some sort of clue," said D.C. But to what, wondered Christina. Her heart started racing. There isn't a mystery, is there? So why a clue?

"Let's go this way!" Grant said. "I found a passage!" He led the others down a dark, narrow corridor. He halted and sharply turned right. Christina could see a small sliding doorway in the wall. She and the others silently sneaked through and found themselves back in the Blue Room.

"I wonder where the Secret Service agent went?" Christina wondered aloud. "She was here when we came through this room before."

"Maybe it's their lunch hour," April said. As soon as she finished speaking, a flash of light blinded them.

"What was that?!" shouted Grant.

"Shh!" whispered Christina. She stared at the back of a person in a black suit who was rushing away from them down the hallway.

"Who is *that*?" asked April.

"I bet it's one of those Secret Service agents–who is going to arrest us!" Grant said nervously.

"No, wait a minute," said Christina. "Why would he or she run away? And what was that bright flash? Maybe this person left that clue?"

Surely Not
A Clue!

A Secret
Passage

"She's right," said D.C. "We should check this room to see if he or she left any more clues."

"Okay," the group agreed, as they split up to search the room.

The Blue
Room

Searching
for More!

6 A TALKING TREE?

Christina searched around the floor on her hands and knees. She gradually made her way to the base of the Christmas tree. Through the window, she could see that the snow was coming down hard. Out of the corner, she spied a flash of black fabric. "Quick, hide!" she whispered to the others.

As soon as the kids had crawled under the bottom branches of the Christmas tree or crouched under couches, a tall, muscular man in a black suit and tie walked into the middle of the room and stood next to the Christmas tree. He took a sweeping glance around the room and ran his hand over his crew-cut hair.

Christina and April were huddled together under the Christmas tree. They silently watched through the branches as the man in the suit put his wrist to his mouth

Searching for More!

Quick, Hide!

31

and said in a low voice, "All clear. Eagle is on the move."

After the man left the room, the kids emerged one by one from their cramped hiding places.

"Whew, that was a close call, huh?" said D.C., sighing with relief.

"Sure was," agreed Grant. "But did that man have a phone cord growing out of his ear?"

"No, goofy, that's the wire to his headset," April explained. "All of the Secret Service agents wear this walkie-talkie thing that allows them to communicate with each other. They have microphones hidden in their sleeves and little speakers in their ears. That's why you saw a 'phone cord.'"

"What about the thing he said?" queried D.C. "You know, the 'Eagle is on the move' thing."

"It might be our next clue," said Christina. "You know, all of . . ." she was interrupted by a strange and astonishing sound.

A voice coming from somewhere around the Christmas tree said, "Good day to you! Good day to you!"

"*What* was that?" the group exclaimed in unison.

"It sounds like we have company," Christina said.

"But we're the only ones here now that the man in the black suit left," responded April.

Quick, Hide!

A Close Call

"Maybe the tree said it!" said Grant. Everyone rolled their eyes except for D.C.

"I think he's right," she said. "There's no one else in here, and I was standing right next to the tree. It certainly sounded like the tree was talking to us."

When D.C. had finished speaking, the voice from the tree (or the voice *of* the tree, for that matter!) said again, "Good day to you! Good day to you!"

The group was so spooked by the talking tree that they ran all the way back to the East Room and slipped back through the secret door into the dim, narrow passageway.

"I don't know which is worse, this creepy place or a talking tree," said Christina.

"I know what's worse," said Grant. "The secret door closed behind us and now it won't open!"

"I don't really care. I just want to find the way out," said April. "Let's go this way." She led the others down the dark corridor.

A Close Call

Aahh! A Talking Tree!

7 SECRET PASSAGEWAY

The children continued down the corridor. Christina looked around her as she walked. Boy, this sure was a spooky place, she thought to herself. The only light in the cramped hallway came from a small, dusty light bulb hanging from the ceiling. The place smelled musty, like a damp, cobwebby old basement. Speaking of cobwebs, there were quite a few along the baseboards, grabbing at their ankles as they passed by.

Suddenly, April–who was at the head of the group–came to a sudden stop, causing the rest of the kids to crash into each other. "Sorry, guys," she apologized, "but I think I found something." She pointed high up on the wall towards the ceiling.

Sure enough, there was a dim reflection like from a mirror. "I think it's a dirty window," said Christina.

Back Behind
The Walls

Creepy
Cobwebs

"Let's boost Grant up on your shoulders so he can see what's out there," April suggested.

"Okay!" Grant agreed enthusiastically.   Christina, however, didn't seem too thrilled.

"Be careful!" admonished D.C., as she helped Grant scramble onto Christina's shoulders. "Now stand up," she said. "April, you be his spotter. That's how we learned to do this trick at cheerleading camp."

"What do you see, Grant?" April questioned.

"Not much. This window is really small," said Grant ,as he teetered on his precarious perch. "Wait, there's a person in there. Wearing a black suit . . ."

"Could it be the same man that was in the Blue Room?" interrupted D.C.

"It might be," Grant replied. "I can't see if it's a man or a woman. They're too far away. Wait, there was just a huge flash! I think someone took a picture of something."

"That explains the flash that we saw in the other room," said Christina. "But I wonder if the Secret Service agent from the Blue Room and the person who took the picture are the same."

"What about Mimi and Papa and Edgar?" asked April.

"They don't seem to have missed us kids yet," said

Creepy
Cobwebs

Another
Flash!

Grant. "They seem too fascinated by this whole White House experience to have noticed the fact that we're not with them anymore."

"That's a relief," said D.C.

"The room is empty now," said Grant. "Do you think we should go in and look around?"

"Sure, I guess," said April. "Here's another sliding door." The group crowded through the narrow opening into the Red Room.

As the children were wandering around the room searching for clues, Christina noticed the man in the black suit and tie at the edge of the doorway. He spoke into his wrist microphone again. "They're out and about," he said in a grave voice. "Yes, I know. We're doing all that we can. We have to get them under control before they can reach the Oval Office."

Oh no, thought Christina, There must be terrorists on the loose! I don't know what else that man could have been talking about. She turned to the others. Their eyes were wide with surprise and fear. They had also heard the man and understood exactly what she was thinking. "We have to go some place safe NOW," she instructed them.

Christina led the group toward the secret sliding door. Before she went into the passageway herself, she

Another Flash!

Into The Red Room

glanced around the room to make sure that no one had seen them. Christina slid through the door and closed it behind her. As soon as she had done so, the lights went off!

Into The
Red Room

Back Behind
The Walls

Looking for clues in the Red Room!

8 LIGHTS OUT!

The kids all screamed. "What happened?" cried D.C.

"I guess this blizzard caused the power to go out," said Christina. "That's the only thing I can think of, unless the terrorists cut the power. Either way, we need to get some light."

Crack! Suddenly an eerie green glow lit up Grant's grinning face. "It's lucky that Uncle Michael sent me these glowsticks from Chicago," he said. He went on to explain to D.C. and April, "Uncle Michael says that these are used by U.S. Marines, like our cousin Matt. There are two kinds of chemicals inside the tube in separate compartments. When you bend the tube in half, it breaks the barrier between the two chemicals and they glow! Isn't that cool?"

"Very cool," responded April. "Just don't get that

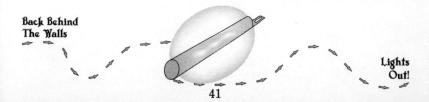

yucky stuff in my hair–I don't want a glow-in-the-dark hairdo!"

"I'm just glad that you have them with you," said D.C., with a sigh of relief.

"Good old Uncle Michael," said Grant.

Using Grant's green glowsticks, the group groped their way along the wall until they found another doorway. They emerged into a large room with a soft carpet underfoot. The glowsticks cast a feeble light onto the wall behind the children. The wall was a pale green color that reminded Christina of lettuce. Christina followed the wall until she found a table with two silver candlesticks on it.

"Hey, we're in luck!" she exclaimed, motioning with her glowstick for the others to come and see. While she waited, Christina read a small placard stating that the candlesticks had once belonged to James Madison, the fourth president, and James Monroe, the fifth president.

The gang gathered around the table. "Okay," Christina said, "Two of us can take these candles, but we have to be careful with them. Look who used to own them," she said, gesturing toward the placard.

April smiled as she and Christina picked up the two candlesticks. "I bet that Mr. Madison and Mr. Monroe would be turning over in their graves if they could see what

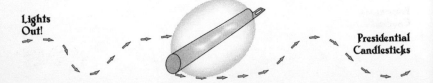

Lights
Out!

Presidential
Candlesticks

we're doing with their silver."

"Don't say 'grave,'" D.C. pleaded. "I'm scared enough already."

"No fair!" protested Grant loudly. "How come the older kids get candles and D.C. and I don't?"

"We'll find you some," promised Christina as she and April walked over to the fireplace. Using their glowsticks, the girls scoured the mantle for matches.

"Here we go," said April, who had found some long matches in a small painted urn sitting on the mantle. She struck one and lit her candle. The warm glow illuminated her brown eyes with an impish sparkle. "Good news for you two," she said, addressing D.C. and Grant. "We found two more candlesticks." She handed them to the younger children and lit their candles using another match. "Be careful with these things," she admonished everyone. "Candles can be very dangerous, so keep them away from yourselves and everything else."

"Now we're ready to find Mimi and Papa and go some place safe," said D.C. As the kids headed toward the doorway, a brilliant flash lit up the dark room, making everyone jump. The kids instead scurried through the secret opening in the wall and slid the door shut after them.

Presidential
Candlesticks

Back Behind
The Walls

"Whew! Must be that Secret Service agent again," said Christina.

"Are you sure that this mysterious photographer and our Secret Service agent are the same person?" questioned D.C.

"You're right," said Christina. "We don't know that yet. We need another clue." As soon as she finished her sentence, April stooped down and picked up a small folded piece of paper that was lying on the floor at Christina's feet. She opened it up. The group gathered around and read:

For Safety:
Go Underground!

Back Behind
The Walls

Another
Clue?

9 DOWN, DOWN, DOWN

"That's funny," said Christina. "That was the same idea that I had. I think that we should get as far down as we can go. That will be the safest place in case any terrorism thing happens."

"But do you think it's smart to go downwards? It sounds like the person who's leaving clues will be in the same place. I'm not sure that we want to find each other," said April, with a shudder.

"Besides, where can else we go?" asked Grant. "These secret doors are great, except we can never figure out how to reopen them. Does the White House even have a basement?"

"All we can do is find out," said Christina.

"Hey, come look over here," said D.C., who was poking around in a far corner of the damp, dark hallway. "I

Another
Clue?

Let's Go
Down

found a staircase!"

The group cautiously picked their way through the gloom, being careful not to singe one another's hair with their candles. Standing coiled in the corner, like a giant snake, was a large spiral staircase. Christina looked up, then down the staircase. It seemed to stretch forever in each direction. "I guess we should go downward," she said. "It looks to me like the best thing to do right now."

"I don't know about that. It might lead to a dungeon," said Grant skeptically.

"We can at least give it a try," said April. So down the group went, slowly and carefully descending the narrow, twisty staircase step by step, with only candles to light their way. Eerie, giant shadows flickered on the walls, following the kids down the stairs. Christina felt like she was trapped in some kind of scary, abandoned lighthouse.

After what seemed like hundreds of steps, the gang reached the end of the staircase. They all stepped out into a dark room. From their candlelight, they could see that the room was small and rectangular. At the opposite end of the room was a door.

"I don't think people are supposed to know that the White House has a basement," said Grant, his eyes bugged out from straining to see in the dark.

Let's Go
Down

A Basement?

"Much less *be in* the White House basement," added Christina.

"Let's see if we can find some place safe," said April. She led the group across the empty room to the doorway on the opposite side. Christina reached up to open the door. It was stuck. She tugged and tugged, but nothing happened.

"It looks like I need some help," she said. Her friends got behind her and pulled.

"This is like tug-of-war," said Grant, who was clearly enjoying himself.

"One, two, THREE!" counted D.C., and on "THREE," everyone gave their hardest pull. The door slowly opened with a suction sound. A blast of cold air rushed past the kids. They sneaked quietly into the chilly, foggy room.

"What is this, the White House refrigerator?" asked Grant.

Christina was exploring, holding her candle up to the walls, which seemed to be made of glass. She pulled open another door in the wall. "It's a florist's shop!" she exclaimed. "Just look at all these beautiful blooms!"

"I had no clue that the White House had a basement, much less a whole flower shop down there," said D.C. in

A Basement?

A Flower
Shop?

amazement, as the group stared at the rows of roses, daisies, carnations, and other flowers of every imaginable color. The next refrigerated case was full of holiday flowers. The potted poinsettias shone blood red in the candlelight. Light reflected off shiny, green, prickly holly leaves and cheerful red berries.

"I guess they're getting stuff ready for the holiday pageant," said Christina.

"What holiday pageant?" asked April and D.C. at the same time.

"Oh, Mimi told me that the White House has a holiday pageant to celebrate all of the holidays that happen in December, like Christmas, Hanukkah, and Kwaanza," explained Christina. "The First Lady chooses a theme. The theme of this year's pageant is 'Animals of the White House Past.'"

"Neat!" said D.C. "I wish we could get invited."

"Right now, the only thing I want is a way out of here. It's freezing!" said April, her teeth chattering.

The kids filed through another hard-to-open door at the opposite end of the flower shop. An orange sign with big black letters was attached to the door with duct tape.

A Flower Shop?   No
                                                  Admittance!

ABSOLUTELY NO ADMITTANCE.
UNAUTHORIZED PERSONS ENTER
UNDER PENALTY OF LAW.

"Now I *know* that visitors aren't supposed to be in the White House basement," said Grant.

"Well, it's our only way out," said Christina. "We're very lost. Maybe we'll find someone who can lead us to Mimi and Papa."

The four friends quietly opened the door and went into the next room–their *next* big mistake!

No Admittance!

The Only Way Out

10 MISSING MENAGERIE

Before the kids could get their bearings, they heard a faraway voice say, "There's absolutely no sign of them. Yes, I'm sure that this is the point of origin. They must have infiltrated the house through the passageways. How did they escape? Negligence on the part of the keeper, if you ask me. No, no sign of Eagle. Yes, sir. I'll keep you posted."

The kids heard footsteps receding into the darkness, then the slamming of a door. They listened carefully for a few more seconds. "I wonder who that was?" said Grant.

"It sounded like the voice of our Secret Service friend," replied Christina. "I wonder why he didn't see the light from our candles and come after us?"

"I know why," April called from across the room.

The Only
Way Out

Who Was
That?

51

"There's a wall that comes halfway into the middle of the room. Lucky for us, he must have been behind it when we came in."

The gang followed April to the other side of the wall. Their feet kicked up dust from the dirt floor. There was a huge open area, with what looked like individual animal pens around the walls. There were two birdcages, four pens filled with hay, two corduroy dog beds, and one cat scratching post. The most surprising sight was a small dugout area filled with water and surrounded by a fence. It was obvious that the room was being used to keep animals–and a big variety at that!

"I didn't know that the President had a whole room just for his pets!" said Grant, in amazement.

"Well, this explains something," said Christina.

"Tell us!" cried April and D.C. in unison.

"You know that first clue that we found? The one that said, 'This place is a zoo?' This place *is* a zoo," Christina exclaimed triumphantly, pointing towards the floor to emphasize their location.

"It seems as if the person leaving the clues wants us to follow them," said April. "You know, they sort of led us to the 'zoo' with their second clue that talked about going underground."

Who Was That?

A Zoo?

"You're right," said Christina.   "I wonder if the terrorists were being held prisoner in the basement. I bet they overpowered their guards and let the animals loose to distract the guards so they could escape," she speculated.

"That could very well be," said D.C. "All the more reason for us to find a safe place—preferably with adults." The group nodded in agreement and set off to continue their search.

The next stop along the kids' unofficial tour of off-limits White House spaces was a room that looked like an ordinary basement. It was stuffed with old toys, unused holiday decorations, clothes, costumes, and all kinds of miscellaneous stuff.   "This looks like our basement at home," said Grant.

"This must be the President's official junk room," joked D.C.

"Or more than one president's junk room," said April. "Some of this stuff looks like it's been here since Teddy Roosevelt was president."

"Well, it's not helping us to just stand here," said Christina. She was about to go out the door when she spied another square of white paper, folded in the middle.

A Zoo?

The Official
Junk Room

The group gathered around to read the latest clue. It said,

> ## Are you
> ## hungry yet?

"OH NO!" they all howled in unison. Everyone had remembered at the same time that the group had planned to meet at the East Gate at noon to go somewhere for lunch. Christina looked at her watch. It read 11:45. Thank goodness, she thought. It gave them fifteen minutes to catch up to the adults and find out just how much trouble they were in. "Come on," she said, addressing the others. "We have to hurry if we want to make it in time, and make sure no one ever suspects where we've been." Later she would wonder why she had ever thought that was possible.

The Official
Junk Room

OH NO!
Hurry!

11 A MAGICAL LUNCHEON

After frantically and hurriedly retracing their steps, the tousled group finally managed to find their way back into the East Room. Racing down the hallway, they arrived back in the Green Room at noon sharp. "Everybody's lips are sealed, right?" said Christina.

"Pinkie swear," the others replied, shaking each other's little fingers.

Christina heard voices coming down the hall from the direction of the State Dining Room. "Here they come!" she said. "Act normal. We'll return to our mystery solving later."

Just before the adults entered the room, the lights flickered back on. "Thank goodness! We can have heat again. It was starting to get really chilly in here," said April.

"There they are!" exclaimed Mimi joyfully, running

Hurry!

Into The
Green Room

over to Grant and Christina and hugging them. "We were just heading to the East Gate. We wondered where you were!"

"I told you they'd be okay," said Edgar, chuckling.

'Just *what* do you think you were doing?" said Papa sternly, glowering down at the kids with his hands on his hips. Uh-oh, thought Christina. We're in for it now. Instead, Papa's face broke into a smile. "Are you kids enjoying yourselves?" he asked.

"We sure are!" Grant piped up.

Why in the world aren't they mad? Christina thought to herself in amazement. She could see the looks on her friends' faces and knew that they were thinking the exact same thing.

"Why didn't you come to get us?" she asked cautiously, still waiting for someone to get angry.

"Well, we were worried at first when we lost track of you," explained Mimi, "but Edgar here assured us that you couldn't get very lost because of the agents posted in all of the rooms. They would make sure that you didn't get lost and see that you stayed out of mischief."

Christina realized that the agents must have been called to look for the animals. That would explain why the kids never encountered anyone in the rooms. Well, except

The Green
Room

Is It Time
for Lunch?

for Secret Service Man. And Photographer Person. Or maybe they were the same . . .

"Mimi's right," Papa said. "We figured that it would be more fun for you kids to look around by yourselves rather than trudging around with us old folks." He gave a belly laugh and everybody joined in.

Whew, thought Christina. She felt like a huge weight had been lifted off her shoulders. The other kids looked relieved too.

Mimi addressed the kids with a smile on her face. "I have a wonderful surprise for everybody!"

"What?" the kids cried, clustering around her, like presents around the base of a Christmas tree.

"You're hungry, right?" The kids nodded emphatically. She continued, "Well, I have some good news and some bad news."

"Bad news first," said Christina.

"As you can see, we're having quite a blizzard," said Mimi, gesturing towards one of the Green Room's large windows. "That means were stranded," she continued.

"Uh-oh," the kids said in unison.

"That means we're stuck here FOREVER!" howled Grant miserably. "We won't be able to get home for Christmas to see Mom and Dad and our house and our

Is It Time
for Lunch?

We're
Stranded!

presents and our . . ." His speech was abruptly ended by Christina, who had clamped her hand over his mouth.

"The good news is," continued Mimi, "that we get to have dinner in the White State Dining Room!"

"Yippee!" shouted April and D.C.

"How'd we manage to get permission to do that?" asked Christina in disbelief.

"It's a long story," said Papa. "The chef had originally prepared lunch for the First Family, but because of this blizzard, they're stranded at Camp David and can't get back to the White House. Since we're stranded in here, and because the chef hated for the meal to be wasted, Edgar volunteered us to help out by eating the meal!"

"But what do we do after lunch? We haven't finished looking around the whole White House yet," said Grant, a look of disappointment in his big blue eyes. Christina suspected it was caused by his desire to continue gallivanting through forbidden passageways of the President's house, searching for clues, missing animals, and mysterious people.

"You can continue your touring after lunch," said Edgar. "But right now, I'll escort you to the State Dining Room where your luncheon awaits." He winked and smiled at the kids, then swept elegantly along the hallway with

We're
Stranded!

To The State
Dining Room

Mimi, Papa, and the gaggle of children following.

At the end of the Cross Hall, Edgar held open the previously off-limits heavy wooden door and allowed them to pass through.

"Ooooohhh!" squealed Mimi and the three girls in delight. Grant just wrinkled up his nose and squinted in disgust. "Too fancy," he said.

The room was filled with a dozen round tables, each covered with a white velvet tablecloth and surrounded by elegant black wooden spindle chairs trimmed in gold. Atop each table, in the center, sat a glorious flower arrangement containing red and white poinsettias and holly in a crystal vase. Between each place setting was a gold candlestick holding a tall white taper candle. A roaring fire crackled in the fireplace. A portrait of Abraham Lincoln hung above the mantle. He seemed to be looking down at them.

"This is just like the inside of a fairytale castle," marveled D.C., as they settled into their chairs.

Christina picked up her menu and read the elegant calligraphy. It announced the afternoon's selections in graceful swoops and curves. She looked down at the bewildering variety of plates, silverware, and glasses. She was a little nervous about knowing which fork or spoon to use for which dish, but she would follow Mimi, who always

To The State
Dining Room

Dining In
Style!

knew the right thing to do in these situations.

The first course, a steaming hot cream of broccoli soup, was served in matching fine white china bowls with gold trim. Papa lifted his glass to make a toast. "To the White House!" he said. Everybody clinked glasses just like they had at Old Ebbitt Grill.

Grant rolled his eyes and said, "Grownups and this toasting thing!" Everyone laughed good-naturedly. Christina could see that he wasn't comfortable in such ornate surroundings. She, however, was having the time of her life.

As she finished her soup, Christina discovered that the bowl had a Presidential Seal printed in the bottom of it, just like the plates. "How neat!" she said. "Personalized presidential china!"

"Each president is given money to buy a personal set of china," Mimi informed the group. "After the president serves his term, his china becomes part of the White House collection."

"Sort of like a personal contribution to the world of dishes," said April, smiling. "If I were president, I would. . . "

The waiter bringing the main course interrupted her. It was roast turkey, served with mashed potatoes and

Dining In
Style

Delicious!

gravy, green beans topped with little slivers of almonds, and cranberry sauce, or as Grant called it, "that red stuff." The group eagerly attacked their plates of food.

When they had finished their generous helpings of delicious turkey, the waiter came back with a plate of fruit and flat circular objects. "What's this?" asked Grant, giving the dishes a suspicious stare.

"It's goat cheese," said Papa. "Just try it. You don't have to eat it if you hate it," he said in response to Grant's squinched-up face of disapproval.

After the fruit and cheese course, the waiter brought out several scrumptious-looking desserts.

"How much food is there gonna be? I'm as stuffed as a Christmas goose already!" cried April.

"But there's always room for dessert," Christina insisted, nudging her and smiling. One at a time, with a great flourish, the waiter lifted a pumpkin pie topped with whipped cream, a warm peach cobbler with melting vanilla ice cream, and a seven-layer chocolate cake off of his tray. After what seemed like an intolerable wait, everyone had their slices of pie or cake or bowls of cobbler.

"Mmm, everything was delicious," said Christina, when everyone had finished.

"Mimi, did George Washington eat cherry pie? Or

Delicious!

Yummy - Dessert!

did Abraham Lincoln eat Log Cabin syrup with his pancakes?" Grant asked, his face full of curiosity. Everyone roared with laughter.

"I'm so full I'll have to waddle through the rest of the house," said Papa. Everyone had another good laugh as they left the table and headed off in their separate directions.

"You kids be good! Don't break anything!" Mimi said, looking over her shoulder and waving.

It crossed Christina's mind to tell the adults about the possibility of terrorists in the White House, animals on the loose, and talking Christmas trees. But they looked so happy, she hated to spoil their day. Besides, what proof did she have anyway?

Yummy -
Dessert!

We're On
Our Own!

12 BACK ON THE TRAIL

"Let's head back to the basement!" Grant said enthusiastically. I want to see if we can find some of those missing animals or terrorists."

"Do you think it's safe?" said April. "I don't want to get mixed up in any dangerous situations."

"Not to mention the trouble we could get into for trespassing in off-limits sections of the White House," said D.C.

"As long as we're careful, I think we'll be all right," said Christina. "It will be a matter of hiding at the right time. Besides, I'm determined to find these animals and terrorists and discover who this Secret Service fellow and our mysterious photographer are."

"Don't forget Eagle!" Grant piped up.

"Well, here goes nothing," said Christina.

We're On
Our Own!

Back To The
Basement

The kids went down the Cross Hall to the East Room. They entered the dark passageway through the secret sliding doorway and were about to go down the twisty staircase when April said, "Uh-oh, we forgot candles."

"You're right," said Christina. "Let's go get them. D.C., you and Grant stay here." April and Christina emerged quietly back into the East Room. They both caught their breath in surprise and shock when they saw the now-familiar, athletic figure of the black-suited Secret Service agent. They hid behind a large wooden table to see what would happen.

The man spoke into his wrist microphone as he twisted his tie with his other hand. "He has been confirmed missing? Are you sure that they checked the Oval Office? The second floor bedrooms and study? Still no sign, eh? This is turning into a crisis situation. Yes, we'll all keep our eyes peeled. Good luck." When he finished speaking, the agent rushed out of the room, a worried look on his face.

Christina and April rushed back to the passageway with their candles. "You'll never believe what we just heard!" April said, excited and all out of breath. She and Christina told Grant and D.C. what the Secret Service

Back To The
Basement

Don't forget
Candles!

When the power goes out . . .

agent had said.

"That leads me to believe that the President is missing," said D.C. "I mean, who else is allowed in the Oval Office and on the second floor?"

"I think she might be right. Good thinking, D.C.," said April, as she put her arm around her little sister's shoulder.

"But I thought that the President and his family were supposed to be snowed in at Camp David," said Grant.

"Maybe that story was a decoy used by the Secret Service to distract any enemies," volunteered Christina.

"True," said April, nodding in agreement.

"Poor Mr. President! I hope the terrorists didn't kidnap him!" D.C. said, wrinkling her forehead in concern.

Kidnapped him or worse, thought Christina to herself. "We've got to get a move on," she said to her friends.

The children trekked through the dark passageway. After walking several hundred feet, Christina noticed a large door with a window in the middle of it. That's unusual, she thought. It looks like it leads to the outside. "Let's see where this goes," she said, motioning for the rest of the gang to follow.

April opened the door, letting in a freezing gust of

Don't forget Candles

Brrrrr!

air. The force of the icy wind almost blew the door off its hinges. Snowflakes caught a free ride into the White House by surfing in on the puffs of chilled air. "Wow, a secret door to the outside!" exclaimed Grant in amazement.

As Christina gazed over the frozen landscape, she realized that this must be the White House's huge South Lawn. She and the others clomped further out into the yard, slogging through mammoth snowdrifts. Suddenly Grant took off, running towards something on the right side of the lawn.

"Wait for us!" D.C. shouted, as she, April, and Christina laboriously picked their way though the treacherous frozen terrain. After what seemed like an hour of trudging through the freezing snow, the girls finally caught up with Grant, who was standing by the edge of a swimming pool.

"Wow, the President even gets his own private swimming pool. Must be the life," said April enviously. The group cautiously peered over the edge of the pool into the frigid water.

"If you fall in there, I'm certainly not jumping in after you," Christina warned Grant, who was leaning out far over the edge and looked precariously close to tumbling into the water.

Brrrrr!

What Is That?

Grant asked, "What is that big greenish thing swimming in the deep . . . "

His voice trailed off in amazement and shock as all three girls screamed in unison at the top of their lungs, "AAAAHHHH!!" The four kids took off running as fast as they could across the slippery, snowy grass, skidding and sliding all the way back to the secret entrance in the side of the building. They rushed inside and slammed the door behind them.

"Did you see what I think I saw?" asked April, panting from the long run in the icy air.

"Good, I'm glad you saw it too. I thought I was losing my mind," said Christina.

"What I don't understand is . . . " D.C. started to say.

"Why there is an ALLIGATOR in the President's pool?" interrupted Grant.

"I have an idea that it might be one of the escaped animals from the basement," said Christina. "It might have found its way out to the pool somehow."

"But how could it survive in that freezing water?" asked Grant.

"And how come the water's not frozen in the first place?" asked April. "There's a blizzard going on out there, for crying out loud!"

What Is That?

An Alligator?

"I bet the pool is heated," interjected Christina.

"Well, don't you just have the answer to everything," said Grant, pouting. He was angry that his big sister had once again stolen the spotlight with her never-ending knowledge.

"So much for the Alligator Incident," said April. "We need to work on finding the President."

Baaaaah! Christina could have sworn that she just heard sheep noises from far away. I must be going crazy, she thought.

An Alligator?   Was That A
                                                               Sheep?

13 WHERE'S THE PRESIDENT?

The group found their way back to the spiral staircase and started heading downward. Christina felt like she was starring in an old-fashioned horror movie. The staircase, with its tall shadows, flickering candlelight, and spooky cobwebs drifting in the drafts of cold air, would be the perfect setting for the scene where the werewolf jumps out and grabs the screaming heroine, she thought with a shudder.

The kids reached the bottom of the staircase and once again pulled open the stubborn door of the florist's shop. As they were crossing to the other side of the room, Grant noticed another small door. "Hey, I wonder where this leads?" he asked.

"There's only one way to find out," April said determinedly, as she bravely stalked through the door.

Was That A
Sheep?

Through The
Florist's Shop

71

As soon as the children stepped into the new room, Christina noticed a delicious scent wafting along on the pleasantly warm air. It was sort of spicy, sort of sweet, a familiar odor that brought back childhood memories. What was it? "Gingerbread!" she exclaimed.

"I knew I smelled something yummy!" D.C. said, rubbing her stomach. "This must be the White House bakery."

"Come look at this, you guys!" Grant shouted from across the room.

The girls rushed over to a long table covered with scrumptious pies, cakes, and cookies. In the middle stood an elaborate gingerbread house, decorated with multi-colored gumdrops, cinnamon red hots, and chocolate kisses. "It's a miniature model of the White House!" exclaimed April.

"Cute!" squealed D.C. in delight.

"Don't even *think* about it!" Christina said, grabbing Grant's wrist. His hand was dangerously close to scooping up some of the white-frosted lawn to sample.

A bright flash from across the room made them all jump.

"There's that darned photographer again!" said April, clearly shaken by the surprise.

Through The
Florist's Shop

Time To Get
Outta Here!

"I think we'd better get out of here now," said Christina. "This person is definitely is on our trail."

"Good idea," the others agreed.

The kids wound their way back through the kitchen to the flower shop. "The thing I don't understand is why someone would be following us around, taking pictures," said Christina.

"Maybe they're collecting evidence to use against us in court for when the Secret Services catches and arrests us," said April glumly.

"Aww, cheer up, sis," D.C. said. "If you ask me, I don't think the photographer is part of the Secret Service. Or even part of the White House staff, for that matter. I bet they're here against the rules just like we are."

"But I bet they're not searching for the President," said Grant. "I doubt if they even know that he's missing."

"They know if he or she and our friend the Secret Service agent are the same person," said Christina. "We don't know if they are or not. Besides, we may even be wrong about the President. He may not be missing anyway."

The group stood looking dejectedly at the floor. This is becoming a big tangled mess, thought Christina. Is it worth going on?

Time To Get
Outta Here!

Big Tangled
Mess

"Well, there's no sense standing around here with long faces, as Papa would say," Grant said, cheerfully breaking the dull silence.

"Okay, we might as well continue," said April. "We've gotten ourselves in this deep."

The kids pursued their trail back to the room where the animal pens were. "Now we know what that funny little pond is for," said Christina, pointing to the small pool surrounded by a fence.

"For the alligator!" said Grant, growling and baring his teeth.

"I wonder where the rest of the animals are?" said D.C., looking around absently. "I'm sure they could do lots of damage to the valuable stuff in the White House."

"I hope not," said April. "It'd be a shame to ruin all of those priceless antiques."

Christina inspected one of the birdcages. She noticed a small scrap of paper attached to one of the perches. It read:

A Big Tangled
Mess

A Clue In
The Zoo?

What was George
Washington's
favorite shape?

"Hey guys, come over here," she said. "This next clue tells us where to go!"

A Clue In
The Zoo?

What Shape?

14 DAMP, DARK, COLD

The group gathered around to read the clue. "What does George Washington's favorite shape have to do with anything?" asked Grant, wrinkling his brow in thought.

"Don't you see?" replied Christina. "Edgar explained to us that George Washington liked oval rooms. That's why the Blue Room, the Yellow Oval Bedroom, and the . . . "

"Oval Office!" interjected April and D.C. together.

" . . . are that shape," continued Christina.

"So the clue means that we need to go to the Oval Office!" Grant exclaimed triumphantly.

"Which means going to the West Wing!" said Christina.

"Wait a minute!" shouted April. "We can't go there! It's strictly off-limits to visitors. That's where the

What Shape?

Which Oval Room?

President works and all kinds of secret stuff goes on. I doubt we could ever get in there with all of the guards and security."

"Plus, that's where the Cabinet meets and where the top-secret Situation Room is located," said D.C.

"Situation Room? Cabinet?" repeated Grant, who was obviously confused by these odd names.

Christina ignored her brother's question. "I still think we need to find the President. What if he's in danger? We might be able to help him," she said to the others.

"Yes," they agreed.

"Well, we need to go to the West Wing, forbidden or not," she continued.

"Okay," D.C. sighed reluctantly. "But if we get arrested, remember that this was not my idea."

"Hey, at least we have a goal and a destination now," said April.

"There's just one problem," said D.C.

"What's that?" asked Christina.

"Which way do we go?" D.C. responded.

"We need to get our bearings," said Christina. Maybe we can find some sort of marker that would let us know where we are. Let's look around and see what turns up."

Which Oval
Room?

To The
West Wing!

The group separated and looked all around the large dirt-floored room for any sort of indication as to where they might be. This is beginning to feel like a wild goose chase, thought Christina. Speaking of geese, I must have animals on the brain. She thought she smelled the unmistakable scent of wet dog.

She saw D.C. crawling around on her hands and knees in a corner. "What are you doing?" asked her sister April.

"I think I might have found something," D.C. replied.

"Let's go see," said Christina, dragging Grant over to the corner.

The gang gathered around D.C., squatting to see what she had discovered. "It's some sort of trap door," she explained. "Help me open it."

She and Christina brushed the dust off of the rusty hinges and pulled. Suddenly the door popped open, throwing Christina and D.C. backwards. They landed in a tangled heap. A huge cloud of dust rose up around them. When the air cleared, Grant ventured over to the hole in the floor and peered down. "There's a ladder in here," he said, his voice echoing in the hollow space below.

"Can you see anything?" Christina asked, trying to

To The
West Wing!

A Trap Door

catch a glimpse by craning her neck over Grant's head.

"I sure can't," her brother replied.

"I think we know what we have to do," said Christina as she looked at her friends.

"I don't want to go down there. We have no clue what might be waiting for us at the very end," said D.C., with a quiver in her voice.

"I'll go down there and check it out," said April fearlessly. "Somebody be prepared to come behind me and hand me a candle."

Slowly, she descended down the ladder. After a few minutes and no word from April, Christina began to get worried. "Are you okay down there?" she called, her voice echoing back from the thick blackness.

"Yeah, I'm fine," came the reassuring sound of April's voice. "Christina, hand me a candle so I can see."

Christina bent over the edge of the hole and reached down as far as she could. "Am I anywhere close?" she yelled down to April.

"Not even," she replied.

"I guess I'll have to climb down there myself," Christina mumbled. She grabbed a candle in one hand and carefully swung herself down onto the ladder. "Here's what we're going to do," she said to Grant and D.C., who were

A Trap Door

What's Down There?

crouched around the opening in the floor. "When I get to the bottom of the ladder, April and I will check out the surroundings to make sure it's safe. If it is, we'll take turns climbing up and down the ladder to get the candles. Sort of like a bucket brigade. Then you two can climb down. Got it?" Grant and D.C. nodded. "Okay," she said. "Here goes."

The rungs of the ladder felt slippery and slimy under Christina's hands, like they were covered with some kind of ancient mud or goo. I'll have to be careful not to slip, she thought, especially carrying this candle in one hand. The further down she went, the colder and damper it felt.

She finally neared the bottom and called for April. "I'm right here," said April, reaching for the candle in Christina's hand. "It's good to see you," she said, smiling in the feeble glow from the candle. "Let's have a look around."

The two girls carefully walked around what seemed to be another series of passageways. Christina could hear water dripping all around her. The air was cold and damp and smelled faintly of mold. A complicated network of pipes snaked its way around the ceiling. She said to April, "This must be part of the White House heating and air

What's Down There?

Lots Of Pipes!

conditioning system."

"I agree," April replied. "It looks deserted."

"Okay, one of us has to go back and get the rest of the candles," said Christina.

"I'll get them," April volunteered.

Once the girls had successfully transferred the rest of the candles to the bottom of the ladder, D.C. and Grant climbed down. The group then assembled to take a look around. "This place makes no sense," said Grant.

D.C. was standing farther down the passageway, staring intently at something on one of the walls.

"What do you see?" asked Christina.

"There's something written on here, but I can't tell quite what it is. The walls are covered with slimy stuff," D.C. said.

April walked over and scraped at the wall. Several years' worth of dirt slid aside under her hand. Christina thought she could make out two white letters written on the wall. Underneath the letters, two red arrows pointed in opposite directions.

"I see what it is!" crowed Grant. "The letter on the right is an E, and the letter on the left is a W!"

"E and W usually stand for east and west," said Christina.

Lots Of Pipes!

East And West!

"Which means that the arrow below each letter points in that direction!" declared April.

"Which means that we can find the West Wing!" shouted D.C. enthusiastically.

"We're almost there," Christina said encouragingly. "Let's 'press on,' as Papa would say."

East and West!

To The West Wing!

15 GO WEST, YOUNG MAN

The children turned left and followed the snaky pipe system–whatever it was–in the direction of the arrow marked W. As Christina trudged along, her shoes made squishing noises on the wet brick floor. Water dripped from the ceiling, making it sound like a room full of leaky faucets. The group slogged their way through the rabbit warren of tunnels and walls.

"This is gross," said D.C., with a disgusted look on her face. "It smells like a nasty gas station bathroom in here."

"Eww, *you're* gross, making a comment like that," said April.

"They certainly don't show you pictures of this part of the White House in the history books," said Christina.

The group walked on for a few more minutes,

To The West Wing!

This Is Gross!

hoping to find something besides an endless tunnel of damp brick walls and floor and an endless network of drippy pipes overhead.

"We're following the Brown Brick Road instead of the Yellow Brick Road," said D.C.

BONG! Suddenly, poor Grant walked headlong into something metal, smacking his head.

"OWW!!" he cried, grasping both of his hands to his forehead.

"Are you okay?" cried the girls, rushing to help him.

"Look at the pretty birdies flying around!" said Grant.

"Oh no, he has a concussion!" cried Christina.

"No, I'm just kidding," said Grant. "I didn't really see anything."

"Well, are you okay?" asked April.

"It really hurt, but I don't think I did any permanent damage," said Grant. "I'll probably be in for a major headache and a beauty of a bruise."

"Good thing you have a hard head," said Christina.

The girls helped Grant stand up. As he dusted himself off, Christina examined the object that he had run into. It was another metal ladder, just like the one they had climbed down.

This Is Gross!

Another Ladder

Things are kind of smelly down here!

"Let's see where this leads us," she said to the others. "I'll climb up first."

Christina carefully ascended the ladder, the palms of her hands and the soles of her shoes covered with some muddy, foul-smelling substance. Even though she was tired, she doggedly pursued her upward climb, rung after slimy rung. Her candle sputtered.

It happened suddenly, caused by a combination of her less-than-alert state of mind and the slippery rungs. Christina lost her grip and footing. She felt the sickening sensation of her feet and hands slipping away from the ladder. She was free falling towards the hard brick floor below. It felt like she had left the pit of her stomach behind her. She fell for what seemed like half an hour, but it was actually only a few seconds.

SMACK! Poor Christina landed on her bottom in a huge puddle of nasty brownish goo.

"Are you okay?" the others exclaimed in surprise.

"I'm fine," she replied. "I wasn't all that far up when I slipped."

"Good," said April. "I thought for sure you'd broken a bone."

Another
Ladder

Whoa!!

"My poor clothes!" Christina wailed, twisting her neck around to check her back. "My beautiful new outfit is covered in stinky, nasty, brown slop!"

"We'll get you to a laundromat as soon as we leave the White House," said April. "I'm sure that stuff will wash out."

"Here goes another try," said Christina, determined to conquer the obstacle before her and finish the climb to the top. It was like riding a horse, she thought. Papa always said, 'If you get thrown, you have to get right back in the saddle and try again.' That's what she was doing, all right, only she hoped that the ladder wouldn't hurl her to the ground a second time. She climbed and climbed, leaving the group on the ground far below her.

"Are you okay up there . . . up there . . . up there?" Grant's voice came echoing up the tunnel.

"I'm fine . . . fine . . . fine . . ." replied Christina.

Almost there, she told herself encouragingly. She climbed a few more rungs and reached her hand above her head. Sure enough, it brushed against a ceiling. As soon as Christina had touched it, a trapdoor sprang open, leaving a square opening. Christina shimmied her way onto the solid ground.

After making sure that she was safe and sound, she

Another Try Up
The Ladder

Finally . . .
The Top!

called down for the others to join her. No answer came echoing back. Oh no, she thought desperately. Maybe they just can't hear me. At least I hope that's what it is. For now, all she could do was wait, shiver, and feel all alone.

April and D.C. stood at the bottom of the ladder, waiting from a signal from Christina. "I hope she's all right," said D.C.

"Do you think we'd be able to hear her from up there?" April asked, turning to Grant. There was no response. "Grant?" she asked again.

"Oh boy, it looks like he disappeared again," said D.C. in despair. "We have to go look for him."

"But how?" asked April." "We can't see any footprints or anything!"

"Look!" cried D.C. "His candle left a trail of wax drippings. That will be an easy way to track where he went."

"Good thinking, sis," said April, as she and D.C. followed the trail of tiny white drops. They took a right turn at a cross tunnel. The trail led them to a wall and then stopped.

"Well, what next?" said D.C. "He couldn't have walked *through* the wall."

finally . . .
The Top!

Where Did
Grant Go?

"I think I know where he went," said April, examining the wall. She yanked at a small protruding knob, and a small door, the size of a kitchen cabinet, came open with a rusty screech. "Look, it's a dumbwaiter," she said to D.C. "It's an old-fashioned way to deliver stuff. Sort of like a mini-elevator. People could put things on this tray, shut the door, and it would be pulled up to a different level of the house. That's how rich people in mansions would get room service."

"Cool! I wish I had one of those in my room," said D.C. "It would be perfect for grabbing midnight snacks."

"I bet that Grant climbed in here and pulled himself up to wherever it leads. We should do the same and see if we can catch him," said April, climbing in.

"I'll come up right after you," promised D.C. as she watched her sister rise up and disappear into the darkness.

Where Did
Grant Go?

Into The
Dumbwaiter

16 An Interesting Situation

Grant climbed out of the dumbwaiter and gazed around the room. It was full of bookshelves and big, comfy sofas and chairs. He slowly walked around, surveying the leather-bound, gold-trimmed volumes. He began opening drawers in one of the small writing desks. He picked up a small, thin object and smiled.

"Whew! What a ride!" D.C. exclaimed as her head emerged from the hole in the wall. She handed April her candle and plopped down on the floor beside the dumbwaiter opening.

"It's not easy, is it?" agreed April, with a sympathetic smile. She and her sister began to investigate the room. D.C. found a light switch and flicked it. To her

There's Grant!

Where Are They?

surprise, the lights came on.

"Ow! My eyes!" she exclaimed.

"After being in that dark tunnel with only candles, electric lights *hurt*," said April. "I guess the blizzard must be causing the power to flicker on and off."

D.C. observed her new surroundings. The walls of the room were painted navy blue and covered with bulletin boards, photographs, charts, and sheets of what appeared to be secret codes. A few individual desks were scattered here and there, each one cluttered with stacks of papers and office supplies. A round table stood in the center of the room, swamped with flashlights, lunchboxes, and more papers. Hanging on a coat rack in the corner were three black jackets. The room gave a we-mean-business, hustle-and-bustle impression. But there was no sign of Grant.

"I bet this is one of the Secret Service offices," said April.

"I agree," said D.C. "Those jackets in the corner look like Gramps' uniform jackets."

"Here's a door," said April, from the other side of the room.

"Let's borrow a couple of these flashlights for safety," said D.C., picking two up off the table in the center of the room. "You never know when we might lose the

Where Are They?   Secret Service
                                                                         Office

power again."

The two silently slipped out of the office into a brilliant white hallway. In front of them on the wall was a sign painted in bold red letters. It said:

WEST WING: NO ADMITTANCE
FROM THIS POINT ONWARD
WITHOUT APPROVED ID.

"We found the West Wing!" said D.C. triumphantly.

"Now what?" asked April. "We don't have a way to get in. We certainly don't have official ID's."

The sisters stood in silence, thinking of a solution to their dilemma. They were interrupted by a familiar, eerie voice chanting, "Good day to you! Good day to you!"

"It's the ghost of Abraham Lincoln!" shouted D.C. as she dove behind her sister for protection, her teeth chattering in fright.

"There! It's coming from that Christmas tree!" cried April, pointing to a small, decorated spruce placed at the end of the hallway.

"Oh no!" wailed D.C. "Another spooky talking tree!'

"Let's get out of here before whatever that *thing* is jumps out and catches us," said April, herding her

In The West
Wing!

Another
Talking Tree!

frightened sibling towards a door at the opposite end of the hallway.

The two dove through the door into another room. "Whew, that was a close one," said April, slumping tiredly against the wall.

"Is there really such a thing as the ghost of Abraham Lincoln?" asked April.

"Tradition says that Lincoln's ghost really does haunt the White House," replied D.C. "Teddy Roosevelt said that he saw the ghost of Lincoln several times during his presidency. Some other former presidents, first ladies, and staff have claimed to have seen him or felt like he was watching them," she continued.

The girls wandered around the room, examining its contents. They noticed that it contained a long table with a telephone at each place, many chairs, and a large TV. Several cardboard boxes were stacked on top of the table. D.C. peeked into one.

"Look at me!" she shouted. When April saw her, her jaw promptly dropped to the floor. D.C. sported a full gas mask, complete with rubber tubes snaking around her head.

"Where in the world did you find that?" demanded April, with her hands on her hips.

Another Talking Tree!

Gas Masks?

"There's a whole bunch of them in this box," D.C. replied.

"You look like a giant bug, or maybe a space alien," giggled April.

"That's it!" said D.C., snapping her fingers. "I knew it all along!"

"Knew what?" her sister asked.

"What this room was," replied D.C. "It's the Situation Room. This is where the President and the members of his Cabinet would come in case of an emergency or a terrorist attack. I've heard that this room has really thick concrete walls, its own communication network, clean air, food and first aid supplies, everything that you would need to make this a really safe place. That explains why I found those gas masks in here," she continued.

"I remember Gramps telling us about it after September 11," April piped up.

"So it's sort of like those underground bomb shelters people had during the 1960s to protect themselves from nuclear attacks," mused D.C.

"Yep, that's right," said April.

"The Situation Room, huh?" said D.C., contemplating the walls. "We're in a pretty strange

Gas Masks?

The Situation Room

situation ourselves."

"Let's continue looking for Grant and Christina," said April. "Standing here isn't doing any good."

The sisters left the Situation Room by a different door and stepped out into a different hallway.

"Okay, this is getting tiring," said Christina to herself, after the she had been walking for several minutes, passing rows and rows of doors that looked just alike. "I'm getting more lost every second. This was supposed to be a *fun* day, *not* a wild winter mystery-solving day."

When Christina finished speaking, she reached a staircase. She started climbing upwards, knowing that this was the only place left to go.

The Situation
Room

Going Up

17 FIRST QUARTERS

April and D.C. walked up a flight of stairs. "I think we must be on the second floor," April said. The hallway was wide and pleasantly lit by big bay windows on one side that looked out on a pretty balcony. The sparkling white paint set off the gold-framed pictures of flowers and little golden tables holding fancy vases and teapots. The sisters passed by several large doors, each one slightly ajar.

D.C. ventured into one room. "Come look at this!" she called to her sister, who was examining a painting of a giant pink rose.

April followed D.C. into a pale blue room. A white iron-frame bed, covered with a blue and-white quilt and several lacy white pillows sat against one wall. A white dresser, vanity, and writing desk completed the room's furnishings.

Going Up

Look At This!

"Hey, this room is just as messy as ours at home are!" said April, gesturing to the dirty clothes strewn around the floor and the posters of movie stars and rock music idols pinned sloppily to the walls. "It sort of makes the President and his family seem more human to know that they can be messy and like the same kinds of things that we do."

"I bet this is the first daughter's bedroom," said D.C.

"You're right," said April. "Check out this picture of her and her father. She gestured to a photo in an elaborate white frame. The smiling faces of the President and his eleven-year-old daughter stared back at them.

"We're inside the President's *house*!" shouted D.C. excitedly.

"We've been in his house the whole time, silly," said April. "I think you mean that we're in the part where the President actually sleeps and spends time with his family and, well . . . lives."

"Let's go see what's in the other rooms!" said D.C., dragging April by the hand into the next room. It was another bedroom, this time with a giant mahogany four-poster bed smack in the middle. The walls were painted a light tan color that accented the elaborate gold brocade bedspread and pillows.

First Daughter's
Bedroom

Presidential
Bedroom

"I guess this is the President and First Lady's bedroom," said April in awe.

"This is where the President *actually sleeps* at night," D.C. whispered in open-mouthed admiration.

April snapped back to attention. "Come on," she said. "We have to look for the others. What if they're in harm's way? We need to make sure they're safe." She and April sped off down the hallway in a westward direction.

Grant was tired. He leaned against one of the bookshelves, turning over in his palm the small pen flashlight that he had gotten out of one of the desk drawers. He shone the beam all around the walls of the study, making the small point of light fly around in patterns, tracing the outline of different objects, even writing his own name.

He shifted the position of his shoulder against the wall. There was a buzzing sound, like that of an electric garage door opener. All of a sudden, the entire wall lurched into motion. It began to rotate slowly, taking Grant with it, all the while making a horrific screeching noise, like nails on a chalkboard.

The turning of the wall slowly revealed a new scene.

Presidential Bedroom

Where Is Grant?

The dim light barely illuminated a large room with a long table in the middle. The table was surrounded by many heavy wooden rolling chairs, which were upholstered in dark brown leather with gold studs. Each chair had a brass plate on the back, announcing the occupant's name and some kind of official-sounding title, like "Secretary of the Interior," or "Secretary of Transportation."

Suddenly Grant heard the squeak of a door opening. He dove beneath the table to avoid being seen.

Christina reached the top of the staircase. Thank goodness it was only two flights high, she thought to herself. I'm too tired to walk much further. She looked to her right and to her left. On her right side, there was a small door with a diamond-shaped window. She walked over and opened it. Outside, there was nothing but a fire escape.

Christina decided to try the door on the left. It was heavy and wooden, and opened with a squeak. She cautiously walked in, being careful not to make any noise. The light from her candle fell on a giant table that stretched across to the other side of the room. There were several wood-and-brown-leather chairs. She stooped under the

Where Is
Grant?

Where Is
Christina?

table to see if anyone was hiding there. A flash of light blasted her in the face, temporarily blinding her, like a deer caught in a car's headlights! She screamed in terror and surprise!

Where Is
Christina?

AAAHHHH!

18 NOT YOUR ORDINARY KITCHEN CABINET

Grant crawled under the table and shone his flashlight directly into the face of the intruder. "AHH!" he screamed.

"AHH!" the intruder screamed at the same time. Through the confusion and fright, brother and sister eventually recognized each other. They hugged, comforted by the company of someone familiar.

"I'm so glad you're safe!" said Christina, looking at Grant's forehead, which was developing a huge black and purple bruise from his collision with the ladder.

"Aww, cut out the mushy stuff," said Grant, disgustedly pushing his sister away, too much of a boy to admit that he was relieved to see her.

"Where have you been?" asked Christina. "I waited for you forever at the top of that ladder."

Grant?
Is That You?

Where Have
You Been?

"I got tired of waiting for you to climb to the top, so I went and found a dumbwaiter. You know, one of those old-fashioned food elevators," Grant explained. "I pulled myself up into the President's study. Then I leaned against one of the walls, and it started to rotate like those walls in scary movies. It turned all the way around into this room."

"Cool!" said Christina. "Were you scared?"

"No, not until you came barging in and scared the living daylights out of me!" Grant exclaimed.

"You should talk!" retorted Christina. "Imagine being in a dark room and someone shining a light right in your face!"

"What happened to you after you climbed the ladder?" Grant asked his sister.

"Oh yeah, after that. I really appreciate your patience, waiting for me to reach the top and all," Christina said sarcastically, tousling her brother's hair.

She continued, "I waited a bit for you guys, then got frustrated and started walking. I really just walked up and down some halls, then climbed a staircase into this room. Nothing exciting, like riding in a dumbwaiter."

"Speaking of this room, just look at all of these heavy chairs," said Grant. "And how come they each have name tags on the back?" he asked.

Where Have You Been?

Where Are We Now?

"Oh, this must be the Cabinet Room," said Christina, smiling.

"Cabinets? But this isn't the kitchen. I don't see any cabinets anywhere," said Grant, looking around with a puzzled expression on his face.

Christina laughed kindheartedly at his confusion. "You silly! The Cabinet is a group of special advisors to the President. Each member is in charge of helping the President out with a particular department. That's what the titles underneath their names mean," she explained, gesturing to the brass plate on the back of one of the chairs. "They also get to keep their chairs when they retire. Their co-workers buy it and give it to them as a gift."

"So what does the Secretary of the Interior do? Does he or she take care of the inside of the White House?" asked Grant.

"Good guess, but no," said Christina. "He or she is in charge of things like national parks and government-owned farmlands and mines. He or she also works to keep wildlife healthy. The Secretary of Defense is in charge of the Army and Navy. The Secretary of the Treasury in charge of the nation's money." She went on to name a few others.

"How'd you know all that?" asked Grant, his eyes

Where Are
We Now?

The Cabinet
Room

wide with surprise at the wisdom of his sister.

"We studied the Cabinet in social studies class at school. You'll learn all about all that stuff someday," said Christina, putting on the airs of a seasoned veteran.

"That's really neat and all, but what about. . ." Grant's speech was interrupted by the return of electricity.

"Hooray for lights!" shouted Christina. She looked around the room and caught a glimpse of her little brother. "Grant, why in the *world* are you standing there in your *underwear*?!" she asked in shock.

Grant grinned sheepishly. "Well, I got covered in dirt coming out of the dumbwaiter. As I was looking around, I happened to run into the White House laundry room. I stuck my clothes in the wash, and I figured I'd pick them up later."

"Only *you* would do a thing like that," Christina said with disapproval, rolling her eyes. How did I get stuck with such a weird little brother, she thought.

"Hey, at least I didn't hang them out to dry in the East Room like they did a long time ago," he said with an impish grin.

"Well, so much for your clothes," she said. "We need to find April and D.C."

"Here we go!" said Grant, opening a door to tiptoe

The Cabinet
Room

Missing
Clothes

through. Just as he did so, the power sputtered again.

"Rats!" cried April, after the girls were plunged into darkness by another power outage. "The stupid electricity keeps going on and off."

"Good thing we kept those flashlights," D.C. said.

"Where do we go now?" April asked in despair. "I was lost enough without the lights going out."

"Calm down," said D.C. reassuringly. "We should probably get as close as we can to the Oval Office. The last time we were all together, we agreed that our task was to find the President. The logical place to look for the President is in the Oval Office. Maybe Grant and Christina will have found their way over there already since they're also looking for the President."

"But what if they stopped looking for the President and decided to get the heck out of this madhouse?" grumbled April.

'Well, what else are we going to do?" asked D.C.

"Get the heck out too?" April said hopefully.

"No, no, no!" cried D.C. "I just know we'll find them somewhere. Come this way." She led her sister back downstairs and into what looked like a well-organized

Missing
Clothes

To The Oval
Office!

office. Their flashlight beams revealed desks lined up in neat rows, each one covered with a tidy assortment of office supplies. Nameplates sat at each one, announcing the owners' names as "Agent Smith," or "Agent Russell," or "Agent Black."

"This must be another Secret Service office," said April. She curiously examined one of the room's walls. It was curvy, instead of straight like the rest of them. It sloped gently outwards into the room, creating a graceful, curvy line across the carpet.

"That's an odd shape for a room," said D.C. She walked over to the wall and pushed on it. All of a sudden, the wall began to swing outward, causing the girls to shriek in surprise and horror.

"It's gonna hit us!" cried April. "Quick, let's go this way!" She grabbed her sister by the hand and dove into the opening created by the mysterious moving wall. To their amazement, the wall stopped moving, and after a brief pause, reversed its direction.

"It looks like we're trapped in this place," said April, as the door closed ominously. "Quick, let's turn off our flashlights so they don't give away our latest hiding place."

To The Oval
Office

Moving
Walls!

19 AN OVALTINE SURPRISE

Christina and Grant stumbled into their new surroundings in darkness. The candle had burned out. "Quick, Grant, where's your flashlight?" Christina whispered. Grant responded by clicking on his borrowed penlight. He aimed the small, bright point towards the floor. It illuminated a plush, royal blue carpet.

"Boy, that's some kind of fancy rug," he said, sweeping the beam of light over the floor.

"Wait a second, let me see that," said Christina, who had spied something out of the corner of her eye. She knelt down and trained the flashlight on a colorful patch of rug to her left. She crawled over and examined it more closely.

The circular patch of carpet was a woven design depicting a majestic eagle wearing a red, white, and blue

Where Are
We Now?

Nice Carpet!

shield and holding an olive branch in one talon and some arrows in the other. The eagle was surrounded by a circle of stars and two stripes, one of red and one of gold. The design was a familiar one. She suddenly recognized it as–

"The Presidential Seal!" she whispered. "Of course! Grant, we're in the Oval Office!"

Grant shined his flashlight beam around, revealing a graceful oval-shaped room painted pale yellow and tastefully furnished with two striped sofas and two pale yellow chairs. Between the two sofas was a fireplace, with an impressive portrait of George Washington hanging over it.

Across the room from the fireplace, stood a magnificently carved wooden desk, dominating the rest of the furniture like a king would his subjects. Behind the desk sat a wide, high-backed, black leather chair, facing away from the children and towards three large windows decorated with elaborate gold drapes. On the left side of the desk, a U.S. flag hung on a staff, and on the right side, a flag bearing the Presidential Seal.

April and D.C. slowly emerged from behind the blue-striped couch, crawling silently toward the center of the room. Just as they were about to shriek with fright, Christina motioned to them to be quiet. They recognized

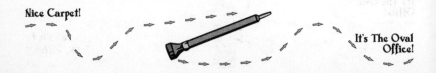

Nice Carpet!

It's The Oval Office!

her intentions and stayed silent.

The faint moonlight coming in the window allowed Christina to see a thin, white tendril of smoke rising from behind the black leather chair.

"The White House is on fire just like in 1814!" she whispered. She rushed over and grabbed the fire axe that was hanging on the wall by the fireplace.

Grant saw what she was doing and snatched up the fire extinguisher and aimed it into the darkness. Then he accidentally pulled the trigger on the fire extinguisher, covering the two sisters in white foam.

"What was THAT for?" April whispered indignantly, wiping the foam out of her eyes.

"Oops, sorry," murmured Grant.

Once again, out of the darkness, came the eerie voice chanting, "Good day to you! Good day to you!"

"AHH!!" screamed all four children in terror.

"WHAT GHOSTS OF CHRISTMAS PAST ARE HAUNTING MY OVAL OFFICE THIS CHRISTMAS EVE NIGHT?" intoned a deep voice, as the big black leather chair behind the desk slowly spun around. The lights flickered back on, and the children gasped in awe

It's The Oval Office!

Who Is In The Office?

at the sight.

Christina stared at the shiny, spotless, polished black shoes, the long legs clothed in black pants, upwards to the impeccably ironed white dress shirt and royal blue tie, to the broad shoulders in the black suit coat, and finally, at the dignified face with kind gray eyes, firm jaw, and neatly combed silvery gray hair.

It was a familiar face, one that Christina recognized from newspaper photographs and TV news shows. It belonged to none other than *the President of the United States*!

"There's the fire!" shouted Grant, aiming his fire extinguisher at a steaming mug in the President's hand.

"Don't point that thing at me!' said the President, shielding himself with his hands. "That's not a fire, just my mug of hot chocolate Ovaltine."

"Oh. Oops," said Grant again. "I guess I'm not cut out to be a fireman."

"Here, give me that thing," said April, yanking the extinguisher out of his hands. "You've done enough damage already."

The President stood up and looked down at the children from his six feet, five inches of height. "*And just exactly what is going on here?*" he said sternly, but with a

Who Is In the
Office?

FIRE

The
President!!

twinkle in his eyes.

"M-m-m-Mr. President . . ." sputtered Grant. "We didn't know you were in here."

"We thought you were missing!" said April.

"Actually I stayed behind in my office to take care of a few last-minute things," responded the President, squinting his eyes.

I'm so ashamed, thought Christina. Here I am covered in stinky brown goo and holding an axe. Grant is in his underwear with candle wax tangled in his hair, and April and D.C. are covered in foam, looking like Abominable Snowpeople. We must look like the terrorists instead of the ones looking for the terrorists. This is *no* way to meet the President of the United States.

Her thoughts were interrupted when six Secret Service agents jumped into the room, guns drawn and pointed at the kids. "DON'T MOVE! HANDS UP!" one of them shouted.

Another agent grabbed a bright red telephone and yelled, "CODE RED! FULL LOCKDOWN!" into the receiver. The kids were petrified, staring at the agents with wide, frightened eyes.

I don't think we're gonna make it out of here alive, thought Christina. In the best case, we'll probably spend

The President!!

CODE RED!

the rest of our lives in prison.

"Is everything under control, Mr. President?" a muscular young agent with a crewcut asked. He moved protectively to the President's side.

"Yes, everything is fine," said the President calmly. "I seem to be having a surprise visit from some of Santa's Christmas elves." He picked up the receiver of the red phone and said, "Cancel that Code Red. It was a misunderstanding. Yes, I'm sure that everything is fine. Smith is right here. Thank you."

"All right people, move out!" the young man shouted to the other Secret Service agents. They put away their guns and filed out of the Oval Office.

The children breathed a HUGE sigh of relief. Christina recognized the young man as the one whom she had seen throughout their wild tour of the White House.

"That's the guy with the phone cord growing out of his head!" said Grant.

"I'm Agent Smith," the young man replied. "I'm with the Secret Service. I was assigned by Edgar to follow you kids throughout the house and make sure you stayed out of trouble."

"Why didn't you ever stop us when we were sitting on the furniture in the Red Room and doing things that

CODE RED!

Christmas
Elves?

we weren't supposed to and going places that we weren't supposed to be?" asked Christina.

"Well, I saw that you weren't doing any real harm to anything, so I just let you enjoy yourselves. Think of it as sort of an early Christmas present," Agent Smith replied, smiling.

"But what about when we went into the secret passageways and down into the basement and stuff? Why didn't you follow us?" asked D.C.

"I couldn't follow you around because we had an emergency. The animals starring in the White House's holiday pageant escaped from their pens in the basement. The keeper turned them loose by accident. We needed every member of the staff to help look for them. That's why I wasn't with you every step of the way."

"So those are the fugitives we kept hearing you talk about," said Christina. "We thought there were terrorists on the loose."

"Thank goodness *that* wasn't the case," said the President.

"We caught all of the escaped animals," said Agent Smith. "We even had a SEAL rescue the alligator from the South Lawn pool."

"Wait a minute," said Grant confusedly. "A seal

Christmas
Elves?

And Seals
Too?

rescue an alligator? I don't think so!"

Agent Smith laughed. "The kind of seal I'm talking about is a Navy SEAL. A SEAL is a soldier who is specially trained in diving and other difficult underwater operations."

"Good day to you!" A bright red, yellow, and green parrot swooped down and perched on the back of the President's black leather chair.

"So that's the talking tree!" shouted D.C.

The President chuckled. "No, actually, that's Captain, my pet macaw."

"Huh?" said Grant, clearly puzzled.

"I can explain," said the President. "Since the White House is pretty much deserted for the holidays (or at least I *thought* it was!), I've been letting Captain roam around as much as he pleases. He likes to perch in the Christmas trees and call out to any visitors he encounters."

"Well, that certainly does explain a lot," said April. "I thought those trees were haunted!"

"No, only by Captain," said the President.

"Meow!" A small sound came from beneath the President's desk. He stooped down and picked up a black and white cat and her four adorable kittens.

And Seals Too?

Meet Captain

"How cute!" exclaimed April.

"This is the cat that is going to be in the holiday pageant," said the President. "She recently had these kittens. We're going to give them to the humane society so they can find good homes."

"*We* have a good home!" D.C. hinted eagerly.

"So do *we*!" Christina said.

"I see what you've got in mind," said the President. "How would you kids each like to take a kitten home as a souvenir?"

"Super!" said D.C.

The children each picked up a soft, cuddly kitten. Christina and April had a small argument over who got to keep the black and white one that was a miniature version of its mother.

"They need names," said Christina. "I think I'll call mine Popular Vote in honor of the President and the U.S. government."

"Mine will be named Major, like a major in the Army!" said April.

"I want to call mine Double S after the Secret Service," said D.C.

"This one is named Seal," said Grant decidedly, holding up his gray-furred, green-eyed kitten. Everyone

Meet Captain

Kittens!

laughed.

"I'm glad that the kittens will be well taken care of and loved," said the President. He knelt down next to the children and petted the mother cat.

Snap! Another brilliant flash blinded the kids.

"What? They're even in the Oval Office!" said Christina.

"What do you mean?" asked a female voice.

Christina looked up at a beautiful, redheaded woman wearing a chic black pantsuit.

"*You're* the mysterious photographer!" said April.

"My name is Ms. Kensington," she said. "I'm one of the White House photographers. I was assigned to follow you kids on your tour so I could take pictures of you admiring the rooms and Christmas decorations. We're doing a big magazine article about children visitors to the White House at Christmastime. I left you clues just for fun,"

"And all the while we thought you were a spy!" said D.C.

"Speaking of Christmastime, tell us about the holiday pageant," Christina begged the President.

"The pageant will be a Christmas Day parade starting at the East Gate and traveling all the way through

Kittens!

The Holiday Pageant

the White House, out the back entrance, and ending on the South Portico," he began. "My wife picked this year's theme of Animals of the White House Past," explained the President. "We wanted to remember and honor some of the more famous First Pets in history. For example, there will be a mockingbird that represents a pet that belonged to Thomas Jefferson, our third president. Its name was Dick. Dick would hop alongside Jefferson when he went up and down stairs. President Jefferson even trained Dick to sing while he played the violin."

"That's one talented bird!" said Grant.

The President continued, "We will have three sheep who represent the sheep that President Wilson kept on the White House lawn during World War I. They kept the grass trimmed while the White House gardeners were serving in the Army."

"Maybe I should trade my kitten for a sheep," Grant (who had the grass-cutting chore at home) grumbled.

"We have a pony who looks just like the one who belonged to Caroline, President John F. Kennedy's daughter," said Agent Smith. "The pony's name was Macaroni, like the one in the Yankee Doodle song. Caroline would ride Macaroni around on the White House

The Holiday Pageant

Lots Of Animals

lawn."

"Cool!" said Christina. "I've always wanted a pony, but I would never name it after *pasta*."

"There will be two dogs, a Scottie and a springer spaniel," said Ms. Kensington, tossing her glamorous red hair. "The Scottie represents Fala, President Franklin Roosevelt's beloved dog. He was perhaps the most famous White House pet. Fala would travel everywhere with the president. He even went on a Navy ship. Fala was missing for a bit, and when the president got him back, lots of his fur was gone. The sailors had cut off pieces of it to keep as souvenirs!"

"Poor Fala! He *really* had a bad hair day!" said D.C.

"The other dog, a springer spaniel, will represent Millie, George and Barbara Bush's dog. Mrs. Bush even wrote a book about life in the White House that was told from Millie's point of view," said Agent Smith.

"What about the cat?" asked April, pointing to the black-and-white bundle curled up on the floor.

"She represents Socks, who was President Bill and Hillary Clinton's–and daughter Chelsea's, of course–pet cat," said Ms. Kensington.

"Why do you have an alligator?" asked Grant. "I've never heard of a First Alligator."

Lots Of
Animals

Alligators!

The President smiled and replied, "The alligator is here to remind us of the creatures that lived in the swamps that once surrounded the White House. Also, President Herbert Hoover's son kept two alligators as pets–and, yes, they did escape sometimes!"

"Well, this certainly has been one of the most interesting–and exciting–days of my life," said Christina.

"Yes?" Agent Smith said. He held his wrist to his mouth and spoke into his microphone. "Edgar, please escort the VIPs to Eagle's outer office."

"That's the *last* mystery that needs to be solved," said April. "Who or what is Eagle?"

"That's our code name for the President," said Agent Smith. "We use it to refer to him instead of saying 'the President' or his real name."

"Hey!" said Grant. "Could you give *us* secret code names? Please!"

The President interrupted, "I can!" One by one he pointed to each child, saying: "Trouble! Trouble! Trouble! Trouble!" The kids laughed sheepishly.

"Now get out of my office!" the President ordered in the same gruff voice that Papa always used when he wasn't really mad.

"You have important presidential business to do?"

Alligators!

Eagle!

Grant asked earnestly.

"Yes," said the President, rising and shooing the children out the door. "I've got to wrap my Christmas presents!"

Eagle

Eagle!

20 AND TO ALL A GOOD NIGHT

The kids moved into the anteroom just outside of the Oval Office. There was a blizzard of hugging and squealing as the four funny friends hugged one another and compared adventures.

"Tell us what happened to you two after I went up the ladder and Grant disappeared into the dumbwaiter," said Christina, after she and Grant had explained their adventures to D.C.

"Well, when we realized that Grant had disappeared, we followed the trail of his candle drippings over to the dumbwaiter," explained April. She continued, "We rode that clanky contraption up to some Secret Service office. From there we went into a hallway."

"Where we saw another spooky talking tree!" broke in D.C. "Then we went into the Situation Room."

What Happened
To You?

Another
Talking Tree

"What's that?" Grant asked.

"It's a safe room, with all kinds of necessary supplies, that the president can go to in case the country is attacked by terrorists, or something else," explained April.

D.C. continued retelling their adventure. "We found our way into the first daughter's bedroom and—you'll never believe this—the President's *very own* bedroom."

"Wow," said Christina. "You're lucky."

April picked up where D.C. had left off. "We were thinking about giving up, but we decided to go back downstairs and check one more room, which turned out to be another Secret Service office. It has a moving wall that let us into the Oval Office," she finished.

"I know *all* about moving walls," said Grant. "I'm never leaning on a wall again! That wasn't smart."

"Speaking of smart, that keeper who let the animals out of their pens sure wasn't the brightest," said April.

"Either that or he had a really *BAAAHD* sense of humor," said Grant, imitating a sheep. Everyone groaned and rolled their eyes at his corny joke.

"I'm sure he'll get a lecture for being so careless,"

First Family
Quarters

The Oval
Office

said Agent Smith.

"So tell us more about the Situation Room," said Christina. There was a knock on the anteroom door, and in walked Edgar with Mimi and Papa.

Christina and Grant ran over to Mimi and Papa and gave them giant hugs.

"Hi Gramps!" said D.C.

"Hello, sweetheart," he replied. He gave the disheveled children an odd look. "What happened to you guys?"

The kids realized that the adults were clueless about their exciting evening. They must have thought that we stayed downstairs in the library and played Trivial Pursuit all evening, thought Christina!

"You kids look very guilty of *something*!" said Mimi. "I'm not sure I want to know what," she added, staring at the dirty children. "And, Grant–where are your clothes? You're almost *nekkid*!"

"Let's just go have dinner at Old Ebbitt Grill. I think it's still open," said Papa, with a sigh.

"Sounds like a good idea," said Grant. "Running around the White House 'nekkid' has made me hungry!"

When Mimi and Papa looked puzzled, Christina explained, "We toured the whole White House, solved the

What Were You
Kids Doing?

Where Are
Your Clothes?

mystery of the Secret Service man, the Mysterious Photographer, and all those animals, *and* we found the missing President all in one day," she said.

Mimi's green eyes got really big. "I don't believe a word of it!"

"We'll tell you about it at dinner," replied Christina. "Are these cats going home with us?" groused Papa.

The President of the United States stuck his head out of the Oval Office and spoke to Papa in his Commander-in-Chief voice, *"OH YES!"*

Everyone (even Secret Service Agent Smith) except Papa laughed.

Mimi sighed, "I'm dreaming of a hot shower and a big, warm, snuggly bed."

"Then check out the Lincoln bedroom," the President shocked her by saying.

"I'm dreaming of a peanut butter and jelly sandwich," wailed Grant, grasping his tummy.

"Well, join me," the President said, beckoning them into the Oval office. "I'll have a platter sent right up! And what are you dreaming about, Miss Christina?" the President asked.

Christina smiled at the President, *her* President.

Now We Have Kittens?

White House Christmas!

We get to stay at the white House!

"I'm dreaming of a White . . . House . . . Christmas."

The President howled with laughter. "Well, I'm the man who can make your dream come true!"

The End

A BOUT THE AUTHOR

Carole Marsh is an author and publisher who has written many works of fiction and non-fiction for young readers. She travels throughout the United States and around the world to research her books. In 1979 Carole Marsh was named Communicator of the Year for her corporate communications work with major national and international corporations.

Marsh is the founder and CEO of Gallopade International, established in 1979. Today, Gallopade International is widely recognized as a leading source of educational materials for every state and many countries. Marsh and Gallopade were recipients of the 2002 Teachers' Choice Award. Marsh has written more than 50 Carole Marsh Mysteries™. Years ago, her children, Michele and Michael, were the original characters in her mystery books. Today, they continue the Carole Marsh Books tradition by working at Gallopade. By adding grandchildren Grant and Christina as new mystery characters, she has continued the tradition for a third generation.

Ms. Marsh welcomes correspondence from her readers. You can e-mail her at fanclub@gallopade.com, visit the carolemarshmysteries.com website, or write to her in care of Gallopade International, P.O. Box 2779, Peachtree City, Georgia, 30269 USA.

Built-In Book Club
Talk About It!

1. Who was your favorite character? Why?

2. What do you remember most about all the things the children saw in the White House? What was most interesting to you?

3. Would you like to be a Secret Service agent? Why or why not?

4. What was the scariest part of the book? Why?

5. Do you think it was a good idea for the kids to go exploring in the White House basement? Why or why not?

6. Who or what did you think the Secret Service agents were trying to find throughout the book?

7. Would you have been brave enough to climb down the ladder into a dark, unknown place? Why do you think all the children were willing to climb down into "the unknown" and no one was afraid?

8. What was your favorite part of the book? Why?

Built-In Book Club
Bring It To Life!

1. What do you do when the lights go out? Talk about all the things you should have on hand in case the electricity goes off at night in your house. What are some reasons that the electricity might go off? Name as many things in your house as you can that use electricity!

2. Can reading make you hungry? Ask book club members to recall the delicious meal the children had in the White House State Dining Room (Chapter 11). Have them list all the adjectives used to describe the meal. Discuss how descriptive words make a scene in a book come alive!

3. Game Day! Select three volunteers to play a game similar to "Jeopardy." Ask the other book club members to write three questions each about the mystery. Give the volunteers a clicker to use when they want to answer the question. Select a host to ask the questions, and see who wins!

4. Ask each book club member to choose his or her favorite room in the White House. Then, ask each student to draw the room, or find pictures of things that might be in the room and put them on a poster. For example, the florist shop would be full of beautiful flowers, or the Oval Office would have a large desk, a fireplace, couches, and chairs.

LOSSARY

antique: a valuable object preserved from the past

banquet: a social dinner, often involving large numbers of people

china: a set of fancy dishes, often used on special occasions

colonnade: a long hallway, usually supported by a series of columns on each side

cornerstone: the first stone of a new building, usually marked with the date

executive: branch of the government involved in making decisions and upholding laws

judicial: branch of government involved with interpreting laws and deciding whether or not they are Constitutional

legislative: branch of the government that makes laws

mansion: a large house with many rooms

portico: a type of porch

solarium: a room enclosed with glass walls

vermeil (pronounced VER MAY): dishes or other objects made of silver covered0 in gold

Recipe for fun: Read the book, take a tour, find the items on this list and check them off! (Hint: Look high and low!!) *Teachers: you have permission to reproduce this form for your students.*

__1. The Willard Hotel

__2. Old Ebbitt Grill

__3. Blue Room

__4. South Portico

__5. Portrait of George Washington that was saved from the White House fire by Dolley Madison

__6. Candlesticks belonging to James Madison and James Monroe

__7. Vermeil Room

__8. Truman Balcony

__9. Washington Monument

__10. Rose Garden

Write Your Own Mystery!

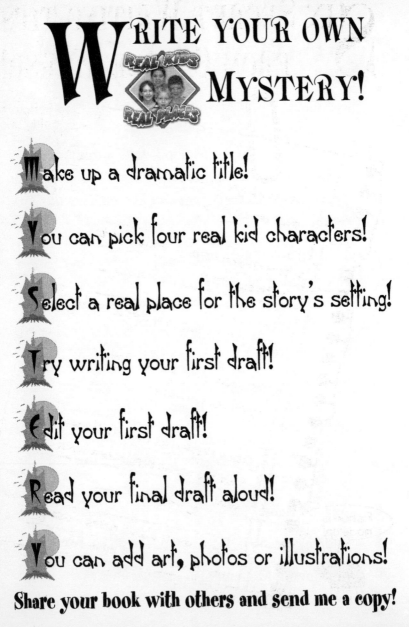

Make up a dramatic title!

You can pick four real kid characters!

Select a real place for the story's setting!

Try writing your first draft!

Edit your first draft!

Read your final draft aloud!

You can add art, photos or illustrations!

Share your book with others and send me a copy!

Six Secret Writing Tips from Carole Marsh!

Non-fiction is factual!

1. Make up good titles – wild and crazy is good!

2. Use strong verbs – action verbs with pizzazz!

3. Edit your work to make it better!

4. Use your own special "voice" to make your work unique!

5. Use a thesaurus and dictionary to find the words that mean what you want to say!

Fiction is made up!

6. Don't worry about rules – use your imagination and have fun!

WOULD YOU CAROLE MARSH MYSTERIES LIKE TO BE
A CHARACTER IN A CAROLE MARSH MYSTERY?

If you would like to star in a Carole Marsh Mystery, fill out the form below and write a 25-word paragraph about why you think you would make a good character! Once you're done, ask your mom or dad to send this page to:

Carole Marsh Mysteries Fan Club
Gallopade International
P.O. Box 2779
Peachtree City, GA 30269

My name is: _____

I am a: ____boy ____girl   Age: _____

I live at: _____

City: _____ State:____ Zip code: _____

My e-mail address: _____

My phone number is: _____

_____
_____
_____
_____
_____
_____
_____
_____
_____
_____

Enjoy this exciting excerpt from

THE MYSTERY ON ALASKA'S IDITAROD TRAIL

1 A LONG WAY FROM HOME

Christina was so excited to get out of school for yet another trip with her grandparents and little brother, Grant, who was seven. She was nine years old and in fourth grade and though she loved school, she always found the 'real' world much more interesting. Her grandmother, Mimi, wrote mystery books and always took Christina and Grant along when she went on trips to do research about her books. It seemed that most every time, Christina and Grant would get into some sort of mystery themselves, giving Mimi even more to write about.

This trip promised to be one of the most exciting yet!

Mimi was taking them to Alaska, 'The Last Frontier'. She was writing a book about the world's most famous dog sled race, the Iditarod.

They had all gotten up very early that morning while it was still dark outside, left Peachtree City where they lived, and flew out of Atlanta's Hartsfield International airport. Their flight to Seattle, Washington took about five hours where they had a layover before leaving for Anchorage.

Christina had to set her watch back three hours to make up for the time difference between Georgia and Seattle.

A layover is just another word for 'hurry up and wait,' Christina thought. It sure seems to take a long time to get anywhere on the big commercial airlines. You have to wait in so many lines and wait to be called to find your seat on the airplane and then wait for the flight attendants to show you the safety rules and then wait until the pilot starts the engines and then wait your turn on the runway before you ever even get a chance to get off the ground.

Christina liked flying in her grandfather's little red plane, *My Girl*, much better. But *My Girl* would never make it all the way to Alaska.

"So, a girl has to do what a girl has to do," Christina muttered quietly.

They hardly had time to get settled in their seats for the last leg of the trip before Grant whined, "When are we going to get there? We've been flying for days."

"Grant, please stop complaining, honey," said Mimi from across the aisle. "I know hours seem like days when you're on an airplane, but we've only got a few more hours before we land in Anchorage, and then we'll be on a whole new adventure. I promise it will be well worth the wait."

"Let's ask the flight attendant for some more munchies," Christina suggested.

Christina and Grant crunched on pretzels and snack mix and gulped bottomless cups of lemonade, as they watched a movie and played card games of Crazy Eights. They giggled at Mimi and Papa as their heads bobbed in tandem, snores erupting from their open mouths.

"This is going to be so cool," Grant whispered in Christina's ear, so as not to wake Mimi and Papa. "We get to explore Alaska and go to the Iditarod."

"Yeah, but Mimi's going to have the most fun." Christina said sulking. "She actually gets to ride along with a musher on the Iditarod Trail in the real race and write about her experience. She's sooooo lucky."

"Musher? What's that?" asked Grant. "Sounds like that squishy stuff with the marshmallows that Aunt Emma makes on Thanksgiving."

"Ha, ha, very funny." Christina scolded. "You know it's the person who leads the dog sled in the races. But, I bet you didn't know that dog sled racing is the official state sport of Alaska," Christina added.

"You always have to know everything, don't you?" Grant grumbled.

"Oh, Grant," Christina said. "I'm just kidding with you."

"Okay," said Grant. "But I bet you didn't know that

Libby Riddles was the first woman to win the Iditarod, in 1985?" He pumped up his chest like a proud rooster and tucked Mimi's Alaskan fact book further under his knee.

"That may be true," said Christina. "But, Susan Butcher is a four-time winner and the first person ever to win three Iditarod races in a row."

"Oh, you think you are so smart. But, did you know that the capital of Alaska is Juneau?" Grant asked.

"I know, but do Juneau?" Christina popped back.

"You are so funny, I forgot to laugh," Grant said, as they both broke into giggles.

A loud snore escaped from Papa's mouth, and the children erupted in laugher.

Mimi snorted awake. "What are you two laughing about?" she asked.

"Oh nothing," Christina said, sneaking a knowing glance at Grant. They both covered their mouths with their hands, unsuccessfully stifling their laughter.

"We will be starting our descent momentarily," the pilot's voice announced over their heads, distracting Mimi just in time.

Christina looked over Grant's shoulder through the small oval-shaped airplane window. She could see the peaks of snow-covered mountains and the telltale aqua blue of glaciers. The sky was clear with billowy clouds that looked like the fluffy cotton that she pulled from the hole in her pillow at night when she couldn't sleep.

"Oh, great!" shouted Grant. "We're here! We're here!